REINVENTING THE EGG

To Win the Game is to Change It

ROGER CUSA

Reinventing the Egg: To Win the Game Is to Change It

First published in 2016 by CreateSpace

Cover design by: Cristina Nogue

ISBN-13: 9781530478323
ISBN-10: 1530478324

REINVENTING THE EGG

To Cristina and our son, Roger

CONTENTS

PREFACE

*Just do things in life the way
other people don't do them.*

—*Sheldon Adelson, chairman
and chief executive officer of the
Las Vegas Sands Corporation*

Reinvent! Challenge the status quo. Create and develop brands that disrupt markets and change how people do things.

Whether you are a marketing director in a global company or the founder of a small venture, the proven path to drive significant business growth and take a big bite of a market is through building brands that create a new competitive space—a new category.

This book is about creating new growth in business through innovation. It is not about incremental ideas or doing something slightly better. This book is about reinventing things, about reinventing the egg.

It aims at challenging the current work and performance of large companies and showing them the opportunities missed when they fail to pursue an effective innovation strategy. And it seeks to provide a vision and structure for smaller brands in order to be successful in the market.

The way I intend to add unique value through this book is by redefining the innovation journey from start to launch in a practical way through more than one hundred examples.

This book is written based on many years of experience in working with marketers and innovators from global brands to smaller companies—cases that I have researched, tested, validated, refined, and contrasted throughout my professional career as head of marketing of innovative brands such as Subway and Ferrero, as well as being an entrepreneur.

I hope you enjoy reading it as much as I enjoyed writing and experiencing it. Far beyond that, I hope to shed some light on the reinvention process and illustrate the essential ingredients for bringing new life to your own brand.

INTRODUCTION

Jerry was a young boy who had just come out of the army when he got his first job in the garment business (specifically the shirting department) in a place called Cornhall Marks. Jerry didn't know anything at all about the garment business. He just arrived in the morning, took a piece of fabric, pulled it, and listened to it. He had no idea what he was pulling. He just saw other people sitting around and pulling pieces of fabrics in different ways. So Jerry did the same.

One day, a salesman who was feeling ill called Jerry and told him, "I have an appointment with the president of Arrow Shirts this morning, and I can't get there. I want you to go. Don't say anything. Don't do anything. Just bring him the bag on my table, take the stuff out, and show it to him. He will give you orders."

The first thing Jerry did was open the bag and take a look at the different fabrics. Jerry didn't particularly like them. So he took them out of the bag and walked around the warehouse to find some more interesting fabrics. Some of them had little cowboys on them; certainly they were a different style. He put those new fabrics in the bag and went to meet Arrow's president. "This is really interesting. I had never thought about doing a whole line of these kinds of fabrics. This is great stuff," said the executive.

The next day, the salesman got back to work, and Jerry gave him the order from Arrow. In fact, the president had ordered lots of stuff. The salesman asked, "What is this? What are these fabrics?"

Jerry said, "These are fabrics I found in the warehouse. I replaced the ones that were inside the bag with them. He loved them."

The salesman replied, "Are you crazy?"

Jerry asked, "What's the matter? What are you upset about? You've got a big order."

The other man said, "These are pajama fabrics you sold him. You don't make shirts out of pajamas!"

And Jerry asked, "Why not? Why not?"[1]

That kid was Jerry Weintraub, who later became a top Hollywood producer of films such as *The Karate Kid* and the *Ocean's Eleven* trilogy, as well as manager of and concert promoter for Elvis Presley, Led Zeppelin, the Carpenters, Frank Sinatra, and Neil Diamond.

Kids instinctively ask, "Why not?" But as we get older, we accept the status quo, and we lose the habit of questioning things—the same way that companies tend to keep doing what they do, even if a small brand appears and threatens their long-term financial position.

Jerry's story is a great way of illustrating how big brands become stagnant or find themselves on the verge of a downward spiral. It is not because they have lost their ability to deliver their core products to their loyal customers; they are still good at it, and their fans will still buy from them. The problem lies in their eroded offerings, which have become irrelevant to the mainstream customer. Now those customers are more attracted to a new category and a new brand that satisfies their needs in a unique way like no other brand does.

Remember Jerry. Ask and answer, "Why not?"

Part 1

REINVENT

1.1. WHAT IS REINVENTION?
A NEW MARKET REALITY

In an era when consumers have unlimited choices, there is no space for creating an average product for an average consumer and selling it the average way. There are innumerable competitors blocking you from getting your voice heard.

Not only are there too many choices, but also, because products and services have become more complex in order to differentiate them, there is a lot of research to conduct from a marketing standpoint. However, there is no time for it. Customers don't have time to educate themselves about minuscule differences. An incremental idea won't make the cut.

At the same time, marketing is seen as a company's final process. Marketing is supposed to promote that average product, to shout about it, and to advertise it so that consumers will buy it. However, that no longer works. It won't take much time for you to realize that your brand or product won't be able to move the sales needle that way. At that point, you will find yourself discounting prices in a bidding war for customers.

Today, brands have to actively reinvent, or they will end up in the fossil layers of business history. Reinvention is at the heart of the issue. New ventures have to create exciting products that people want to engage with and are willing to share the news about with others. If you don't imagine your product on the cover of a national newspaper, featured on TV news, or as a subject that people are talking about, then you might have to reconsider it.

The goal is to create a product that reinvents the established norms. A marketing campaign starts with creating a product or product feature with the potential to spread like an idea virus.

Zappos, the online shoe retailer, is a clear example of this. Zappos challenged the status quo by asking: Why can't people buy shoes online? How can a company attract people to buy shoes online without trying them? What if they don't fit? Before Zappos, the online shoe industry didn't show any promising signs of taking off. The problem was that companies were taking customer service for granted. The whole shoe industry was so used to providing average and poor customer service that no one thought of it as a product feature. The news is that customer service can be part of your product and also part of your marketing. Zappos knew that.

So Zappos created the most unbelievable customer service. While other online retailers such as Shoebuy and OnlineShoes offered a thirty-day return policy, Zappos jumped into the market with a 365-day return program, offered free shipping on all returns, and even displayed a 1-800 number on every single page of its website, generating huge press attention and positive customer word of mouth that spread like fire online and offline. Zappos reinvented online customer service and the shoe industry.

No matter what business we're in, the more we try to be logical in our reasoning and base our decisions upon established knowledge, the more likely we are to drive our business into mediocrity and go unseen by our target customers.

Reasonable strategies will guide you through the most crowded path, the one with more competitors. Unreasonable strategies will lead you to unconquered territories. Reasonable strategies are predictable. Unreasonable strategies are surprising and unbeatable. Being reasonable is a shield. It can protect you, but you won't win a battle. Being unreasonable is a sword. Reinvention is about being unreasonable; that's because it challenges what is established.

The reasonable man adapts himself to the world: the unreasonable one persists in trying to adapt the world to himself. Therefore all progress depends on the unreasonable man.

—MALCOM GLADWELL, WRITER FOR NEW YORKER MAGAZINE, BEST-SELLING AUTHOR, AND SPEAKER

REINVENT, DON'T INVENT

Let's forget about the perceived image of innovation as that moment in time when someone comes up with a great idea out of nothing—that moment in time that is commonly illustrated with a light bulb over someone's head.

Every new product and every new thought has evolved from other ideas and experiments. Michele Ferrero, founder of the Ferrero Group, was aware of it. As he stated, "Do you know why kids love Easter eggs so much? Because they have surprises inside…. So do you know what we have to do? Let's celebrate and give them Easter eggs every day."[2] And this is how Kinder Surprise was born—a result of observing today's consumers and building on an existing idea. That's what I call reinvention.

Reinvention is about creating a new solution to a problem by matching existing technologies to current and emerging consumer behaviors. The goal is not to invent or to become a pioneer, which is what people tend to associate with innovation. The goal is to take advantage of an existing technology, move it one step further, and find a new and unique solution to a problem.

The result is a product that people will talk about—a product or business so exciting and unique that it will spread among a community of consumers.

Take one of Walt Disney's first early successes and a key turning point in his career, the animated short *Steamboat Willie*. The cartoon had a combination of two key ingredients to be successful in the movie and cartoon industry at that time: unique characters like Mickey and Minnie and a lighthearted story. However, what really set his short apart was sound. No one had ever done a piece of animated work with such complex sound integration, which was called synchronized sound. This might sound very technical, but in fact it was just a group of people banging on pots for the percussion and using whistles, bells, and other instruments to record at the same time that the picture was running.

Walt didn't invent the cartoon industry. Walt didn't invent the sound film. What Walt did was get an existing technology, which was sound, and blend it with animation. And in this way, he reinvented the modern cartoon with "Mickey Mouse the Sound Cartoon," which became the first pillar of his business empire.

Inventors invent. Businessmen reinvent.

ALL IS AN EVOLUTION

Who invented the steam engine? James Watt.

Who invented the light bulb? Thomas Edison.

Who invented the car? Henry Ford.

We tend to simplify history by assigning an innovation to a sole person, and that is never the case, including the examples above. All is an evolution. And like in any evolution process, there are many people involved: engineers, businessmen, designers, scientists...you never really begin from scratch. So you have to take inspiration from previous projects that have succeeded and ones that have not. It is going to be the most valuable R&D lab you can have—and at a fraction of the cost.

According to the Nobel Prize-winning economist Edmund S. Phelps, there is an interactive connection of ideas over distance and time. The ideas that a society generates come from their combination and multiplication. The same way, the economist-novelist Daniel Defoe shows us with his book *Robinson Crusoe* how difficult it is to generate ideas without exposure to society from which to take inspiration.[3]

No one knows about FingerWorks, the gesture-recognition software, but everyone is familiar with the Apple finger trackpad that millions of people use every day. The company, which was founded by John Elias and Wayne Westerman in 1998, produced a line of multitouch products such as the iGesture Pad, which has defined the foundations for the gestures we use every day with smartphones and tablets.

FingerWorks was acquired by Apple in 2005, an investment that allowed Apple to leapfrog any competitor trying to develop the technology from scratch. Entrepreneurs may not be able to buy a whole company, but certainly you can dig deeper into how these innovative companies are using a new existing technology and building on their successes and failures.

The same thing happened with Google Glass, the groundbreaking product that allowed users to interact with their mobile apps and functions through futuristic-looking glass frames. Google became the reinventor, the one who took an already existing concept and brought it to the mass market. However, before Google, there were many companies developing their own versions. For instance, in January 2002, a company named X-River Technologies launched the Xybernaut, a $1,499 wearable computer that had a one-inch screen positioned in front of the user's eye. In 2005, they filed for bankruptcy. Some experts at that time said the product was too bulky and that the batteries didn't last long enough.

On top of that, they just didn't have the right technology platform and solid user base in place such as Google has nowadays.

There are countless extremely innovative products that are currently being developed and even sold. The problem is that they are just being ignored—sometimes because they might be ahead of their time, sometimes because they didn't have the right platform, or sometimes because the product didn't deliver the expected benefits for consumers.

Identify those pioneers in the industry and capitalize on their knowledge to develop your own reinvented version.

Apply past learning everywhere.

IMPROVING PEOPLE'S LIVES WITH A REINVENTED SOLUTION

> *Create things that hopefully can make a difference*
> *to other people's lives. The reason you're in*
> *business is to make peoples' lives better.*

—*Richard Branson, founder of Virgin Group*

We constantly hear "I have a great product, better than the competitors'. However, sales are not going well. I have to find a better way to promote it."

The problem is that it is not about being better; it is about coming up with a new solution that solves a current problem and improves people's lives ten times more than any other alternative.

Andrew Grove, president and CEO of Intel Corporation, minted the idea of only creating technologies that would be ten times better than any other alternative. You may have heard this concept before; however, the original idea comes from Andrew Grove's book *Only the Paranoid Survive.*[4]

The way I see it is that achieving a 10 percent product improvement will actually mean that you are probably doing the same as everybody else—definitely not a game-changer strategy. And there is no way your company will capture significant market share from that effort.

Instead, focus on creating excitement around a consumer solution that doesn't exist or that is perceived as ten times better than any other alternative in the market. Ask the right questions, and find a new answer.

You need to rethink problems entirely. You need to reinvent. You need to challenge what is established. Most people around you won't share your vision. However, this uniqueness is the reason that reinventors find the opportunity where others do not.

Build a brand that makes a difference.

THE BRANDS THAT REINVENTED THE EGG

Reinvention is about creating a new solution that is ten times better than any other existing alternative by matching available technologies with emerging consumer behaviors. But more importantly, the new offering needs to create a new category in the market. And one brand needs to manage and lead that new category.

A brand won't be able to set itself apart from competition with an incremental product improvement since something that is just slightly better will only deliver low-growth profitability or no growth at all in a mature and stagnant category.

Certainly many big and complacent companies don't spend time reinventing their products. Many? I mean *most* companies don't reinvent—frequently because they are not aware of the connection between reinvention and growth. But in other cases it is just because they are too busy printing vouchers to increase next week's sales and are clueless about giving people a reason to buy from them.

However, throughout history, there has always been a group of entrepreneurs that understands the idea of challenging the status quo and the opportunity of reinventing a market.

These are the Johns, the Nicks, the Patricias, the Mels, the Walts, the Bens, and the Jerrys—people who were once called outsiders and underdogs. Now they are known as market leaders and visionaries. I am talking about game-changing reinventors John Lasseter, cofounder of Pixar; Nick Woodman, founder of GoPro; Patricia Ziegler and Mel Zenler, founders of Banana Republic; and three names that don't even need introductions, Walt Disney, and Ben and Jerry.

They have all reinvented the egg. They have reinvented something that was apparently unchangeable, something that was a given by its very nature and that no one has questioned before.

On one hand, reinventing the egg is a metaphor that can be applied to any industry. But on the other hand, it can be done literally.

Yes, you can. How can this possibly be done? You just have to remove the hen out of the equation.

For instance, the company Hampton Creek Foods has created an egg that improves people's lives because it helps them avoid cholesterol entirely. Anyone will have the opportunity to make cookies or cakes with a reinvented egg that doesn't make them take in any cholesterol. And this reinvention even improves animals' living conditions because these eggs are not laid by hens in small cages, where they are packed in body to body and don't see the sun in their battery-cage facilities.

So how has the company solved this problem? It has created an egg made from plants and even improved it at a deep molecular level. It has made the egg cheaper and healthier with the same taste and without the environmental consequences of building and maintaining big production facilities.

The opportunity is huge: 1.3 trillion eggs are laid every single year around the world. This is a mainstream product for everyone in the world to enjoy through different applications: sauces, dressings, baked cookies, cakes, and many new ones to come.

So I hope I have shown the size of the prize for reinvention. Now the question is: what is the process from start to launch?

If it is possible to reinvent an egg, you can reinvent anything.

THE REINVENTION PROCESS

So where do you start in reinventing the egg? I've written this book so that you can read it from cover to cover and follow the logic of the three-step reinvention process, but it is worth delineating the steps briefly here. To appreciate the stages, it helps to consider what must be accomplished in each one.

1. Reinvent: Identify a problem that has consumer traction. In other words, find a problem that people are inefficiently solving by their own means. Then solve that problem in a new way. Give to a community of customers an unexpected and extraordinary added value that improves their lives. However, the reinventor does not invent a product or service; he or she evolves, perfects, and frames it in a way that creates a new competitive space, a new market category that makes competitors irrelevant.

2. Build: Create a solution so unique that it creates a new category in the market. Do it with your current resources, and start small in order to validate the initial idea. Focus on the set of benefits that customers will really value. At the end of the day, you need to determine whether you can transform that idea into a product, whether consumers will buy it and stick with it, and whether you will be able to sustain it over the years by generating a profit.

3. Connect: Engage with a passionate, networked community who will praise your new product. The key is to build a company one step at a time, from the bottom up, through grassroots marketing, by creating a valuable content strategy, and by spreading the story of your company to generate credible buzz on traditional and social media.

Throughout this book, I'm going to challenge you to break with some common and popular business ideas and practices. You can't solve new consumer problems by using fossilized principles or by just being slightly better than your rivals. The goal is not to win at someone else's game but rather to change the game to one that you can win.

It is time to begin this journey.

1.2. SOURCES OF REINVENTION
THINK LIKE AN OUTSIDER

We need to bring in outside people so we keep throwing ourselves off balance.

—BRAD BIRD, ANIMATOR, DIRECTOR,
AND PRODUCER AT PIXAR

People within an industry tend to read the same magazines, attend the same conferences, and study the same successful business cases. Whenever you find a convergent belief, challenge it.

Ferran Adria, the chef at El Bulli restaurant, which was considered the best in the world for five years and was most known for its innovative deconstructive cuisine, once said, "If I had studied in a prestigious cooking school, I know I wouldn't have done what I have done. I believe that if you go to a place that teaches you what exists and how things are supposed to be, you don't question things."[5]

By having this outsider view, you will be able to identify the gaps and opportunities that others inside the industry won't see. You have to bring fresh eyes to your business as an entrepreneur or as a marketing executive for your company.

You could have put the top one hundred executives in the consumer electronics industry in a room for a week and told them to come up with the next camera. I am certain that no one would have proposed a company like Instagram or GoPro, two very successful companies that have reinvented the photography business. Incumbents just don't have the fresh outsider perspective to develop game-changing products.

Why is it so difficult for incumbents to reinvent? Fear. Fear of cannibalizing their existing brands. Fear of challenging their core business. You are probably aware of the countless number of studies and tests that a new product has to pass before the marketing director can recommend its launch. That is because the only important thing is that it delivers incremental sales growth, maybe delivering 2 percent growth to the total revenue. But that is safe. And safe in the corporate world is good.

In the '70s, Sony became what Apple represents today, an innovation powerhouse—especially when, in 1979, Sony introduced the Walkman in Japan. This product was a mobile audio-cassette player that allowed anyone to enjoy music anywhere, and it put the Sony brand in everyone's hands and minds. The Sony Walkman was the brainchild of the two company founders, Masaru Ibuka and Akio Morita, and it represented the birth of a whole new category: "This is the product that will satisfy those young people who want to listen to music all day. They'll take it everywhere with them, and they won't care about record functions. If we put a playback-only headphone stereo like this on the market, it'll be a hit."[6]

However, when the MP3 market appeared, Sony was unable to retain its dominance in the mobile music market. Instead, with their iPod and iTunes system, Apple reinvented how music was bought, stored, and played. What had happened to Sony? Sony's MP3 player was not was not able to deliver a user-friendly device in terms of functionality, but, most importantly, Sony's software division wanted to protect the royalties from their music division, which again shows that the fear of cannibalizing an existing revenue stream can blind a company from focusing on the future and from building a sustainable position in the market with a reinvented and relevant offering to consumers.

Like fish that can't conceive of a world not immersed in water, most of us can't visualize business ideas that don't correspond to the norms of our own experience.

Question your inheritance. Reexamine your heirloom beliefs.

INSIGHT OF ONE

Good products are built by people who want to use it themselves.

—DAVID KARP, FOUNDER AND CHIEF EXECUTIVE OFFICER OF TUMBLR

The common and structured approach to getting valuable consumer insight is to start the process by hiring a research agency to conduct a detailed and scientific study that identifies current attitudes and behaviors of consumers concerning an existing category of products. The results of the study are considered valuable sources of ideas for multinationals to develop new products aimed at gaining incremental revenue.

Is this the only way? Not at all. There is an alternative way to start getting valuable insight from you alone. You can identify the problems you encounter; you just have to be conscious about it.

For that reason, an entrepreneur and a marketer need to be in the field. Instead of sitting down and thinking about it, get up and do it. Do what you are most passionate about. And observe.

Hotmail originated from the insight of one. When two entrepreneurs named Sabeer Bhatia and Jack Smith created their web-based database start-up, they had to work from the client's office, a place where they could not access their e-mail accounts because the company's firewall prevented them. It was a problem they personally faced and for which they found a new and unique solution: to create a web-enabled e-mail that could be accessed anonymously through any web browser. They launched this e-mail start-up on the Fourth of July of 1996, coinciding with Independence Day to celebrate a new way to get e-mail and be free from the existing Internet service providers. It was called HoTMaiL (as in HTML, the standard language used to create websites). On New Year's Eve 1997, Microsoft acquired Hotmail for $400 million.

TripAdvisor originated from an insight of one. The start-up founders, Steve Kaufer and his wife, Caroline, were planning a vacation to an island. It was between 1998 and 1999, so the web was already considered a source of information. So the couple started to look for opinions about the island and the hotel the travel agency had recommended to them. There was nothing, only some chat rooms that didn't recommend the area because it was unsafe. That was an eye opener. Any person could benefit from other people's experiences and recommendations of a specific hotel, airline, or anything related to travel. People wanted unbiased, unofficial, and personal opinions to help other travelers make the right choice—an insight drawn from their own experience, which they realized, afterward, that millions of people also shared.

As an entrepreneur, you should validate products on the market, but first you have to build them for yourself. If you are passionate about cycling but you don't like the energy bars on the market, why not come up with the product you would love to eat? Gary Erickson, founder of Clif Bars, thought this way and used his mother's kitchen as a product lab to transform the energy bar from a taffy-like snack to a tastier bar that cyclists wanted to eat.

The key is to realize that whatever happens to you as an individual, it always happens to thousands and thousands of people around the world. I always say, "If you have thought about it, many other people will have also." Hence, by starting to identify the problems you encounter, you will be able to find many sources of ideas. It might seem obvious, but the reality is that the majority of times we don't see the problems or opportunities. First, because we solve them inefficiently and just cover the problem. We just work our way out of them and keep going with our daily lives. And, second, even if we are aware of them, we just don't come up with new and unique solutions.

So identifying an insight from our own individual experiences as consumers is a valid starting point. In fact, it is the starting point for many successful companies: Spanx, Geox, Nike, TripAdvisor, YouTube, Facebook, and GoPro, just to mention a few.

All of these entrepreneurs identified and solved their own problems and, as a second step, realized that millions of other people were in the same situations as them and embraced their new solutions.

The first customer is you.

TRACTION

*Innovation is hard because 'solving problems
people didn't know they had' and 'building
something no one needs' look identical at first.*

—*Aaron Levie, cofounder and
chief executive office of Box.*

Traction is as important as the foundations of a new building. Without it, whatever you build on top of it will crack and fall.

But what is traction? Traction is, for instance, a group young people putting a mobile phone on speaker mode to listen to music. It is an inefficient way of solving a problem. It is people using a product a certain way inefficiently.

That is the traction an entrepreneur or a consumer electronics company should identify in order to build the next groundbreaking product and at the same time creating a new subcategory in the market.

This is the foundation upon which Jawbone built the innovative Jambox wireless and Bluetooth speaker for portable and outdoor use. It is a speaker that can be paired with mobile phones in any outdoor or indoor setting, with far better sound quality than a mobile phone on speaker mode. This is also a new subcategory that got more and more crowded in a matter of months with competitors such as Bose, Beats, and LG launching their own versions.

The next thing is happening right now. Don't look to the future. Look for current consumer traction.

As time passes, consumers from different countries will encounter the same problems. Global consumers are not isolated because our lives tend to be more and more in line with a common monoculture—especially because digital media has increased awareness of brands on a global scale at the same time that corporations are expanding their frontiers to add more sales to their bottom lines. Therefore, in many cases, a given consumer traction will be scalable and valid in other parts of the world.

McDonald's was built on the growing traction that people wanted indulgent food—fast. This was a trend that began after the end of World War II and expanded quickly across the United States and also globally.

Going back to the first example, consumers can now find iPhones everywhere and, in the same way, will use it to listen to music with friends, underlining the same consumer traction in many different places. Therefore, seizing on this is a significant worldwide business opportunity if you are able to solve the problem in a unique and relevant way.

There will always be local consumer traits to take into account. But what is clear is that the stakes are now higher than they had ever been before when it comes to creating products that can spread globally.

As marketers, we must recognize that there is an increasing convergence of culture around the world, which represents an opportunity to move a small brand into a mainstream market and into a global brand over time.

Observe what people are solving in inefficient ways.

OPPORTUNITY WINDOWS

Traction could be considered as an isolated event. It only identifies a consumer need. The magic happens when a new technology appears that allows individuals or companies to solve that inefficient problem better than any existing alternative. And that second part of the equation is what is called the opportunity window.

An opportunity window is an early moment in time when a new technology appears on the market, allowing companies to create new offerings and innovative solutions that change consumer behavior and that become ten times better than any other alternative. It represents the inception of a trend.

In the 1967 classic film *The Graduate*, there is a scene at a cocktail party in which an experienced business executive called Mr. McGuire tells a young Ben Braddock (played by Dustin Hoffman), "Just one word: plastics." That scene became a cultural touchstone still very present nowadays. While at that time, the key word was "plastics," we could apply it to the many opportunity windows throughout history. Now you could substitute the words "mobile apps," "share economy" (with examples such as Airbnb), or "the Internet of things," referring to the infinite number of objects that can be enhanced by connecting them to the Internet. And that is what is called an opportunity window.

When the plastic industry was born in 1868, it was not an immediate success in the mainstream market. As always, there were the pioneers and then the reinventors, who spread the use of plastics in every industry. It all started when a manufacturer of ivory billiard balls created a competition to find a substitute for ivory at a time when the material was in a serious shortage. A printer named John Wesley Hyatt from New York won the prize, ten thousand dollars in cash, with a product named celluloid, a material that he did not create, because it was already trademarked in 1872. Instead, he acquired the British patent from an English professor who didn't find a market in the 1850s for the thin, transparent, and moldable film.

Hyatt did not stop at manufacturing billiard balls made of plastic; he saw the potential of the material and began commercializing celluloid collars, cuffs, combs, and jewelry. Then George Eastman introduced celluloid photographic film in his Kodak cameras in 1889. Then Thomas Edison expanded the use of celluloid strips as the key material to record motion pictures. And in 1937, the chemist Earl Tupper, who worked at DuPont, left the company to take advantage of the opportunity window of polyethylene or plastic. In 1945, he introduced the bathroom tumbler; a year later, he presented the tumblers in different colors: lime, crystal, raspberry, lemon, plum, and orange. It was a new and unique product line for the consumer that became an instant hit in the market.

Opportunity windows are key moments in time when new categories are created and when business empires are built. Opportunity windows do not appear from nowhere; they are an evolution, as had happened in the plastics industry.

So as an entrepreneur or a business executive in a big corporation, you have to identify new technologies that have recently entered a market, track them, and understand how they can change consumer behavior and how you can use them to create a new consumer by offering a product ten times better than any current alternative.

Opportunity windows become the starting point of long-term consumer trends. But it is not uncommon to see companies misinterpret those trends and confuse them with short-term fads, something that could put the whole project at risk from the very beginning.

Build during opportunity windows.

TRENDS VERSUS FADS

Am I building my business upon a trend or a fad? What is the difference, and why does it matter?

Let's start by distinguishing them. Faith Popcorn, marketing author and founder of the consulting firm BrainReserve, says that fads are about products, whereas trends are about what drives consumers to buy products. She also adds that trends cannot be created, only observed.[7]

The big point of difference is that trends demand substance and action. Trends are based on a growing change in consumer behavior. On the other hand, fads tend to be linked with products that don't necessarily respond to a particular change in consumer behavior or solve a consumer problem. They tend to be something very typical from fashion-related industries and something that eventually will lead to an extreme rapid growth in a short period of time before bursting.

This is what happened to Crocs, the colorful rubber shoe manufacturer that became an overnight success after some Hollywood celebrities were photographed in them. That made the firm's stock soar to $75 in October 2007 and then fall to $0.79 eighteen months after the fad had ended. The company did recover from that fall and is back in business again, aiming at a broader target market, which they were able to capture through a new shoe range built around their unique rubber pattern. However, the company has never gotten back to its initial hype.

Given this context, you will preferably want to build a business on top of a robust trend, not a fad, as long as your goal is to build a sustainable business and not one with a short-term exit strategy.

That is why it is so important to distinguish between trends and fads at the beginning, as they lead to two very different business paths.

Fads materialize around a product that gives momentary joy. They grow fast and vanish. Trends are rooted in a change in behavior. They grow strong over time and stay.

The last thing you want is to burn too brightly and too fast, only to fizzle out in a few months.

GOLD IS *NOT* WHERE YOU FIND IT

Beware of how you interpret trends.

The media loves covering successful entrepreneurial stories that attract online readers because people like to share and be informed of global business successes. Research institutes publish white papers about the growth opportunities in certain industries so that business executives can make rational decisions about where to invest their money. So when two or more fingers point in the same direction and say, for instance, that the app world is going to grow tenfold in the following years, what happens is that more people will jump into that market and build an app just because some have said that the industry is going to grow.

Now the question that very few people ask is "Will my company be successful even in a growing market?" The majority of people just take for granted that entering a growing market will be synonymous for success, and that is very misleading and dangerous.

Reinvention, creating a new, unique, and relevant solution to a consumer problem, is all about consumer traction, no matter whether the industry is growing or not. I agree that mobile apps have become an opportunity window, but that doesn't mean it is the only market in which to build something unique and new. A highly successful company named Nest reinvented the fire alarm and the thermostat with a unique design and user-friendly products and software, the same way James Dyson reinvented the vacuum cleaner.

There are a quarter of a billion thermostats in the United States alone that will need to be upgraded over the next few years, and there are only a handful of thermostats that are able to provide energy savings. There may only be one as beautifully designed, cheap, and easy to install and use as the Nest thermostat.

You probably don't know the story of Jesse Lasky, but you probably know the empire he founded, Paramount Pictures. [8] His life before founding Paramount Pictures was a constant struggle to make his own way, including some business failures. One of his failures illustrates the case of picking up on a market that would apparently do well, but after some digging, he realized it was all an illusion.

Lasky literally went to look for gold after reading an ad in a newspaper that said, "New Gold Discoveries. Cape Nome. Bigger than the Klondike or Yukon." News of fortunes from the frozen dirt of those two regions in Canada had been making headlines, so he thought that Cape Nome would be a huge opportunity. He booked a passage on the first boat to sail north to Cape Nome on a three-week trip to Alaska. Gold was not lying on Cape Nome's beach; he had to lease part of the beach. So he contacted a local businessman who led him to a small spot, gave Lasky a shovel and a miner's pan, and told him to dig until he found black sand. Lasky dug with all his energy, scooping the black sand into the miner's pan. Then he carefully moved the pan in circular motions until some bright colors started to appear on the bottom. According to Lasky, it was probably five dollars' worth of flour gold. And it didn't take him long to calculate that at this rate, he would be able to make fifty thousand dollars a month. So Lasky signed the lease and the day after hired some more people to help him dig and speed things up. After a couple days of digging, they weren't finding the gold he expected. Someone asked him, "Ever heard of salting?" At that time, it was a common practice to hide some gold under the sand to convince an overly ambitious and naïve person that he would find gold on the beach. It was clear that Lasky could have bought gold at a cheaper price than it was costing him to lease the land and hire those people to dig.

Nowadays, everybody is talking about how "easy" it is to build and sell an online business, for instance, making millions in the process. Don't select a market just because it is talked about and on trend; select it because you can bring a new, unique, and relevant solution to consumers.

You are solving a consumer problem. You are not seeking gold.

MACRO TRENDS VERSUS MICRO TRENDS

The second thing to watch out for is that there is an infinite number of trends, which happen to cross over and apparently contradict each other.

Within the world of trends, there are significant differences that can be misleading. The key is not only to identify macro trends but also, and even more importantly, to identify micro trends—trends that are highly relevant for a targeted group of people.

For instance, pursuing a healthier lifestyle is a macro trend that is shaping the innovation and marketing departments of global consumer product companies. Companies are now investing in launching sugar-free chocolates, hundred-calorie snacks, or antioxidant drinks. However, that could mislead us into thinking that consumers no longer want tasty and indulgent burgers, which is not the case. For instance, the American burger chain In-n-Out is growing massively by focusing on made-to-order burgers and using high-quality ingredients and processes such as nonfrozen beef patties, a micro trend inside the burger industry. Therefore, macro trends can be a misleading source of insight. Macro trends could lead a successful burger chain such as In-n-Out, which has a very limited menu with burgers, fries, and shakes, to expand its offerings by incorporating the traditional version of a salad or wrap, a move that would immediately kill its focused position of offering quality and made-to-order burgers. Instead, In-n-Out Burger has responded by offering their famous burgers wrapped in hand-leafed lettuce instead of a bun, calling this "protein style," an initiative that will maintain its core equity on quality and made-to-order burgers and improve its relevancy with millennial customers by offering them a healthier option.

There is never one only macro trend that shifts an industry. There are numerous trends that will clash with smaller trends, and the majority of them will be valid and present an opportunity for a new brand.

Don't stick with the most obvious macro trend. Dig deeper, and you will find a great number of micro trends that can still represent a huge business opportunity that your brand can own.

Dig deeper. Never settle for the obvious.

IDENTIFYING THE TREND BUT NOT DELIVERING THE RIGHT SOLUTION

Even if you correctly identify a trend and the consumer problem, there is an infinite number of solutions you can come up with. Identifying the trend only represents 1 percent of the equation. Nowadays it is fairly easy to access consumer and market data that will point you toward a predictable future direction. However, creating a unique solution around it and successfully introducing it to the market is a much more complex task, especially because it involves creativity and operational excellence blended together.

Decades ago, premium coffee was a growing trend, but neither Maxwell's or Folger's coffee found the winning consumer solution to capture this market. However, two companies with two very different approaches were able to do so: Starbucks with their retail approach and Nespresso with their patented capsule system to enjoy high-end coffee at home.

The health trend has been a huge business shaper in the last years; however, very few have been able to fully grasp the market. In the quick-service restaurant (QSR) industry, Subway became the king by associating its brand with eating and living fresh, whereas the great majority failed to create a relevant and appealing solution to the consumer.

Today no one remembers, but in 1991, McDonald´s introduced the McLean Deluxe burger in an attempt to create a healthier burger. The first problem with this burger was that men were turned off by its name and image. Its second problem? Taste. Even the TV commercial said, "McDonald´s explodes another myth. Low-fat and delicious? Can't be done. Introducing McLean Deluxe, made with a 91 percent fat-free beef patty. McLean Deluxe will blow you away. Terrific! It can't be low-fat."

Instead of blowing people away, it just drove them away. That is what happens when you remove fat and substitute it with water. According to consumers, the burger tasted awful. So it is no surprise that it failed big time in the market.

Identifying the trend is just a small and obvious part of the marketing proposition; the difficulty resides in creating a relevant and effective consumer solution.

Identify a trend, create your vision, and test your solution until it is the right one.

REINVENTION IS ABOUT IDENTIFYING TALENT

If you give a good idea to a mediocre team, they will screw it up. If you give a mediocre idea to a brilliant team, they will either fix it or throw it away and come up with something better.

—ED CATMULL, PRESIDENT OF PIXAR ANIMATION STUDIOS AND WALT DISNEY ANIMATION STUDIOS

Even the Walt Disney Company, which I have previously been praising, also became an incumbent at one point in time. Years after Walt passed away in 1966, the organization still had success inertia, and things were running smoothly.

In 1984, Roy E. Disney brought in Michael Eisner as CEO and chairman of the board. And Eisner brought in Jeffrey Katzenberg as head of the studio. They had worked together and had a very strong and positive relationship at Paramount Pictures.

However, everything changed for the Walt Disney Company in 1994. Two big events indicated that the wheels were coming off their car. It was the perfect storm.

On one side, Jeffrey Katzenberg had been gaining too much media attention and power within the organization, which Eisner didn't like at all. The tipping point was the day Frank Wells, the president and chief operating officer of Walt Disney, died in an unfortunate helicopter crash on Easter. Eisner refused to promote Katzenberg to president and fired him later that year. Remember that Katzenberg had been the gemstone of the great Disney's turnaround. Under his management, they produced *Who Framed Roger Rabbit?* (1988), *The Little Mermaid* (1989), *Beauty and the Beast* (1991), which was the first animated feature film to be nominated for an Oscar, *Aladdin* (1992), and *The Lion King* (1994) and were even responsible for revitalizing the Star Trek franchise with the launch of the *Star Trek: The Motion Picture* (1979).

Where does all this bring us? Katzenberg joined forces with Steven Spielberg and the music producer David Geffen; with the financial support of Microsoft's cofounder Paul Allen, they created DreamWorks, the second computer-generated animation studio that entered that growing market, which Disney had refused to develop years before, having been too focused on traditional and already known animation techniques and technology. Disney lost the talent that shook the animation industry.

There is a different example with the same outcome. In 1979, a new employee named John Lasseter joined the Walt Disney Feature Animation firm to start working as an animator. He breathed and embraced the corporate culture even before working as an animator. Lasseter had already worked at the Disneyland theme park in Anaheim, California, and even studied at the California Institute of the Arts, which Walt Disney founded in 1961.

But even his passion for Disney did not prevent Lasseter from seeing that something was missing there. They had been creating great movies without any significant innovation for the past ten years. And he couldn't have been more right because, years later, in 1985, Disney had finally hit bottom with the release of *The Black Cauldron*. The twenty-fifth film in the Disney Animated Classics cost $44 million to produce, and it only grossed $21.3 million in United States. It even was beaten at the box office by *The Care Bear Movie*, which generated $22.9 million domestically. Disney's offer was definitively not a classic for the audience.

The company needed a change. And it had the opportunity back in 1983, when Lasseter created a computer-animated movie at Disney. He was inspired by the techniques that the *Tron* movie (1982) had used and quickly saw its potential in the animation business. With computers, production studios would be able to create three-dimensional characters and backgrounds like no one had seen before. So he convinced his colleague Glen Keane (one of the most prominent illustrators at Disney, who created the characters for *The Little Mermaid, Beauty and the Beast*, and *Tangled*, just to name a few) to create a feature animated film based on a book called *The Brave Little Toaster*, by Thomas Disch. The story was about five electric appliances—a toaster, an electric blanket, a radio, a vacuum cleaner, and a desk lamp—on their quest to find their original owner.

After months of working on the project, it was time to pitch it to his superiors and high-level Disney executives: animation administrator Ed Hansen and head of Disney studios, Ron W. Miller. They both asked Lasseter if the film had been cheaper or had been done faster with computer-generated animation. The answer from Lasseter was neither. CGI or computer-animated imagery was not about doing things faster or cheaper; it was about creating new and unique visuals.

Later that day, Lasseter received a call from Hansen to come down to his office. Lasseter was fired on the spot. And this became one of the biggest failures for Disney in the long run.

Lasseter went to work at Lucasfilm Computer Graphics group with the guru of computer-generated imagery, Ed Catmull, and the visionary George Lucas. The company became Pixar in 1986, when Steve Jobs acquired it after being forced out of Apple. And for Lucas, this allowed him to focus on creating entertainment properties rather than tools.

Eight years later, in 1995, Disney had to convince Pixar to distribute and market its hit movie *Toy Story* because it had not been able to develop this technology from within.

In summary, two talented executives who were fired from the Walt Disney Company were the ones who reinvented animated movies, a new category that gained millions of viewers and fans and grossed billions in the box office.

The Walt Disney Company had only one way to participate in this new growing category: buying their stake—first by partnering with and later by acquiring Pixar for $7.4 billion. The Walt Disney Company had lost its magic and clearly had become an incumbent that could only compensate for its lack of vision with cash.

The Walt Disney Company, once the greatest innovator in the entertainment business under Walt Disney's leadership, became one of the biggest incumbents.

The moral of the story is simple. Focus on identifying the key people whom an organization needs to hold on to, even if they are challenging the status quo and your company's products. Reinvention is not about one person's effort; it is about nurturing an innovation culture that attracts talented people and keeps them engaged and inspired.

Identify and keep the John Lasseters and Jeffrey Katzenbergs as they are the greatest sources of continuous innovation and business growth.

Find good people. Set them free.

1.3. LEADING WITHOUT COMPETING

The best way to reinvent with success is to create a new category in a market. Most companies spend their time measuring themselves against their competitors, something that has two consequences:

Lower margins: Customers find it very difficult to distinguish all the offers in the market. The existing category has only evolved with incremental innovations. So when all companies follow the same innovation ambitions and strategy, the only way to escape is a price reduction, putting more pressure on margins and on the short term. In other words, companies get stuck in the past and on trying to squeeze the most of their product portfolio. They are all looking at what their competitors are investing in on TV, which is already the past, and then act based on it.

Lower growth: Companies obsessed with competitors are usually focused on benchmarking competitors' products, on matching their specs, and, if successful, maybe even being perceived slightly better by consumers and eventually obtaining incremental growth to keep up with the average growth of the market.

Instead, companies should be built around new categories. The strategy should be focused on establishing and developing an upcoming category instead of focusing efforts on the competition.

Go where others aren't.

CREATE A NEW CATEGORY, NOT A NEW BUSINESS

As an entrepreneur, you have to think whether you want to create a new company in an existing category crowded with dozens of competitors or establish a new category to deliver value to consumers as no one has ever done before. Do you want to be part of the existing environment, or do you want to reframe it?

Do you want to create a better cola drink like RC Cola did with its RC100—a caffeine-free and sugar-free soft drink—or do you want to create the energy drinks category like Dietrich Mateschitz did with Red Bull?

In April 1980, when RC launched its caffeine- and sugar-free RC100 cola, it was alone in the market. In 1982, you could find their product around United States, but still no competitors entered the ring. No one seemed to follow. It was not until July 1982 that Pepsi entered the caffeine-free category and not until April 1983 for Coke. So RC Cola had between a two- and three-year advantage.

However, by 1990, there was a perfect negative correlation to the order of entry in the market and their market shares; RC had the lowest share, and Coke had a market share that exceeded the combined shares of RC Cola and Pepsi caffeine-free products. Coke compensated for its late entry with a great advertising budget, a strong distribution network, and leverage to get high visibility on the supermarket shelves.

Strategically speaking, just adding a product feature to an existing category was far too risky. RC should have created a new drink that established a new category instead of creating a slightly better cola drink because, by its building a new category, the already existing market leader would not have had the credibility or awareness to compete.

Instead, Red Bull invented a new space where none of the big players were competing and hadn't had the credibility to compete. Mateschitz had the vision of turning an underdog drink, Krating Daeng, which was already being sold in Thailand in the '80s, into a mainstream product and a new global drink category. Nowadays in the United States, Red Bull still enjoys a 43 percent shareof the energy drink market, with an aspiration to sell one billion cans in the country.[9]

In this case, Coke could not just put in or remove an ingredient from their cola to compete with Red Bull. It had to create its own brand from scratch, and nowadays it is still very far behind. Its only way to get a greater stake of the market was by acquiring or partnering up with other, smaller competitors like Monster energy drink. Coke totally missed the boat on energy drinks. It did not have the vision to identify the growth in that category or the knowledge to compete in such a category, which was completely defined by Red Bull. Red Bull won by changing the rules of the game.

In 2011, the branding expert David Aaker illustrated this point in his book *Brand Relevance*, explaining the importance of establishing a category rather than competing in an existing one.[10] Aaker studied the beer market in Japan, a market dominated by two companies, Kirin and Asahi, and whose market shares had only been marginally changing for more than three decades. The market share was a static number that had only significantly changed on four occasions: three changes caused by introductions of new subcategories and a fourth by repositioning an existing subcategory.

The most representative case was the introduction of Asahi's new Super Dry brand. The new product was launched in 1987, and it represented the creation of the superdry beer category, a beer that delivered a sharper and fresher taste without the usual aftertaste of products offered by competitors such as Kirin. The beverage was framed as a sophisticated product with a Western image targeted to a younger generation of beer drinkers.

In 1986, Asahi had only a 10 percent market share that was in steep decline. However, thanks to the Super Dry launch, in a few years, Asahi was able to capture 25 percent of the market. Bear in mind that in the United States, it took the light-beer category eighteen years to capture the same market share of 25 percent. That clearly shows the success dimension of the new superdry category and its leader, Asahi. Even its competitor Kirin referred to Asahi Super Dry as a "game-changing product with resounding success."

What did Kirin do? First, it redefined its flagship beer, Kirin Beer, to Kirin Lager Beer to better describe the attributes of the product. In this way, it would be able to guarantee its position in the lager beer category. Its previous name, Kirin Beer, was rather generic in a market that was increasingly offering a wider variety of beers differentiated by taste. So it was ensuring a position in a declining beer category, a highly defensive strategy.

Second, Kirin launched new products that tried to capture these new flavors and diverse taste preferences demanded by beer consumers, including entering the dry-beer space with its own Kirin Draft Dry Beer. However, the company lacked credibility in this new space to overcome the success of Asahi.

Asahi continued focusing all its efforts on promoting the superdry category, and in 2001, it achieved 37 percent of market share, consequently becoming the number-one brand in Japan.

Rather than competing in the same beer subcategory where a strong beer aftertaste was appreciated by consumers, Asahi created a new field where the rules to win were completely different. Consumers were seeking a dry and fresh aftertaste that they could only find in Asahi Super Dry. Asahi had created the new rules, and Asahi won.

To win the game is to change it.

CATEGORY CREATORS DON'T SEEK MARKET SHARE

The definitive study in favor of pursuing market share to drive profitability is the one conducted by Harvard professor Robert D. Buzzell and published in 1975. The study named *Profit Impact of Marketing Strategies (PIMS)* was a large-scale research program with the goal to identify and measure the determinants of profits in businesses. The main result of the study was that the main determinant of business profitability is market share. So companies that enjoy a high market share will be more profitable than smaller-share rivals, a credo that dominated among big corporations at that time.

However, there is a huge flaw in this study. Market share is about the past. It is lifeless and does not consider future competitors that will have a significant impact on the profitability among all the players in an industry or even challenge their survival probability.

Nowadays, this is still more preeminent with big-bang disruptors. New brands that create new categories, such as the Amazon Kindle or the Tesla electric car, started competing with high-performance products and by targeting the mainstream consumer from the start, which meant that they were turning the competitive strategy upside down. Their products achieved a leadership status from day one, and no incumbent could challenge them.

So don't focus on competing for market share; concentrate on building a unique solution and category that are highly valued by consumers. Then results, including market share, will follow.

The future will be shaped by brands that create new categories.

DEFINE THE NEW CATEGORY WITH FOCUSED INNOVATION

Not having a clear goal leads to death
by a thousand compromises.

—*Mark Pincus, cofounder, chief executive*
officer, and chairman of Zynga

Herb Kelleher, CEO of Southwest Airlines, explains how important it is for a category creator or reinventor to define the category driver. One day, Tracy, a marketing executive from Southwest, came into his office to ask, "Our surveys indicate that the passengers might enjoy a light entrée on the Houston to Las Vegas flight. All we offer is peanuts, and I think a nice chicken Caesar salad would be popular. What do you think?"

Kelleher responded, "I can teach you the secret to running this airline business in thirty seconds. This is it: we are *the* low-fare airline. Once you understand that fact, you can make any decision about this company's future as well as I can. So does your proposal help the business to become the unchallenged low-fare airline? Because if it doesn't, we're not serving any damn chicken salad."

A company that establishes a new category has to define and focus on the main driver that will build credibility and consideration among a group of customers. Keep the main thing the main thing. Every decision you make needs to get the business closer to achieving its unique value to the customer.

Take, for instance, the case of the hamburger chain that reinvented the restaurant industry, McDonald's. Their first hamburger stand was so focused on speed of service that customers could only order from a narrow selection: hamburger, cheeseburger, French fries, milk shakes, and sodas. Their mission was to serve the fastest, cheapest, and tastiest hamburgers in the neighborhood. So everything they did had to be done to come closer to that goal.

They broke almost every rule in the business. At that time, people went to a restaurant to choose among steak, shrimp, fish, chicken, or salad. So it defied logic at that time. But that is reinvention in its purest state. It's so unique and new that it challenges the status quo.

Ask what the category stands for. Then focus.

REINVENTING AT DIFFERENT LEVELS

Reinvention is not only about the product itself; anything surrounding the product can become a source of value to the consumer. So you have to question every single consumer touch point because each of them can be a source of reinvention and a source of uniqueness to make your company stand out from the rest.

It's what Ferran Adria, one of the most innovative chefs in the world, has been known for: deconstructed cooking. The idea is simple; it is about creating dishes that are physically unlike the originals but with all the same or even more flavors preserved. The same thing happens with reinvention; you have to deconstruct each part of the offering you are providing or the current market is providing and try to change one layer at a time, adding value that resonates with consumers and makes your business unique.

Ice cream is an $85 billion market worldwide, in which the majority of brands are focused on launching new ice-cream flavors. You can have plain strawberry, vanilla with macadamia nuts, or even the Nestlé dark-chocolate flavor. That was ice cream before Cold Stone, the company that reinvented ice cream by focusing on the elaboration process and on the serving of the product.

People can choose from a wide range of fresh fruit, sauces, cakes, cookies, and dried fruits to put on their ice cream. The ingredients are all put together over a frozen board made of granite stone (hence the name Cold Stone) and are amazingly mixed with two metal spades to give you customized ice cream made of fresh ingredients in an entertaining atmosphere. People walking down the street stop to see how these ice creams are mixed with such talent; it reminds me of the technique used at Benihana restaurants.

Cold Stone reinvented ice cream by focusing on the preparation of the product. No one offered that solution in the market. The company has been growing since its launch, boosting demand for a product with frozen sales for the past decade.

The world is full of companies that have reinvented at other levels. Here are some examples:

1. Product

A candy manufacturer can develop two products—a new chewing gum with peppermint flavor and with small peppermint particles inside that provide five more minutes of freshness or mint strips that dissolve instantly in your mouth without having to be chewed and freshening your breath by killing 99 percent of bad-breath germs like Listerine did.

This last product is no longer a chewing gum. The chewing gum is out of the equation. This delivers a new solution to a current problem: to freshen your breath instantly, which is the real consumer benefit.

2. Experience

Richard Branson has always been driven by finding new ways to deliver a great experience and customer service through his numerous businesses under the Virgin brand. Virgin America has become the pinnacle of this innovative vision.

From the start, he knew there was an opportunity to fix the broken consumer proposal from the traditional airline players by creating the number-one customer-centric airline with an elevated flying experience. Virgin Atlantic was actually the first to offer individual TV screens and a choice of channels to passengers in all classes in 1991.

Since then, Virgin America has elevated the customer-experience bar in the industry. Virgin America has created the first inflight social network called Here On Biz to take advantage of those serendipitous travel moments when people with complementary business interests can make their dream contacts. Virgin has also put together a group of thirty frequent flyers and entrepreneurs called VX Next that acts as idea generators. And it even reinvented the inflight safety video with a music video that looks more like an MTV hit and has been viewed more than 11 million times on YouTube.

Their achievements have been recognized by many industry experts and media as one of the most innovative companies in the world. Not bad for an airline company that operates outside of the three global airline alliances.

3. Consuming Occasion

Domino's Pizza created a new place of consumption: people's homes. It was the first company that invested in creating a delivery platform to serve customers at home, hence creating a new subcategory: home pizza delivery.

4. Framing

Red Bull was capable of redefining a market where the only attribute that counted was flavor. Red Bull introduced the energy drink category worldwide, offering the extra energy that modern lifestyles demanded.

5. Advertising

GoPro, Red Bull, and TED conferences forgot about traditional TV advertising in favor of using content marketing. Not only did they create unique products, but they also reinvented advertising by connecting with audiences in a new, engaging way. They all created sharable content that people were willing to watch and spread.

6. Price

Vente-privee.com reinvented the luxury business at a lower price level by offering top clothing and accessories brands at a fraction of their cost. In order to compensate for the impossibility of trying on the clothes before buying them, vente-privee.com offered prices for premium brands that no one had ever seen before. There was a time when the luxury industry was promoted through the four senses: smelling the leather, touching the textures and fabrics, seeing the collection in a beautifully designed store, and hearing brand-related music there. That is until vente-privee.com entered the industry by only utilizing one sense: the sight to see the incredibly discounted prices the website offered.

All of the above are non-mutually exclusive levels of reinvention. On the contrary, new ventures frequently reinvent at more than one level. What all these examples have in common is that they are providing new and unique solutions to consumers that represent new categories in the market.

Every brand contact point presents an opportunity to reinvent.

HOW IMPORTANT IS TECHNOLOGY IN INNOVATION?

Technology is a key driver in marketing and innovation. The most revolutionary changes have resulted from the emergence of new technologies. But as John Lasseter said, "Computers don't create computer animation any more than a pencil creates pencil animation. What creates computer animation is the artist."

It is the marketing executive or the entrepreneur who needs to challenge technology and put it at the service of its brand purpose. Technology will enable and inspire, but it will never manage a brand or lead a new category.

However, not all reinventions closely depend on new technology. There are three different grades of involvement. New technology can interlace, empower, or become a support for a new product.

Interlaces

WhatsApp and Facebook are companies that are totally interlaced with technology. In fact, they are built upon a new technology and are highly dependent on it to progress. However, there are companies that are less obvious that are also interlaced with technology. GoPro is a sound example. I don't believe that the portable and mountable camera could exist without new platforms such as YouTube in particular and social media in general. Their HD Hero camera has become the must-have for any sportsperson willing to share his or her experiences on YouTube. It organically grew in this channel; otherwise, it would have become another small and compact camera. Still today, the success of the HD Hero camera comes from creating a product with which you can share your videos within a digital community.

Empowers

In 2013, the fast-casual bakery and café chain Panera Bread was experiencing a decline in sales growth of 2.3 percent versus a 5.7 percent sales increase in 2012—a decrease that the chain partly attributed to potential customers leaving the store without ordering because staff members were too busy to serve them.

In April 2014, Panera unveiled that it had found the key ingredient in the recipe for success, Panera 2.0, a series of integrated technologies to improve the guest experience. It is a project that the company had been testing and developing since 2011.

The new strategy had been designed to satisfy customers' needs based on their ways of enjoying their food on the go and eating in, as well as enhancing the power of personalization.

With it, Panera was not only trying to solve the speed-of-service challenge but was aiming at giving a better guest experience. People could either order their food via the Panera app on a mobile phone or via one of the in-store ordering digital kiosks. Customers would then go into the store and pick up their orders from a designated shelf; dine-in customers would have their orders delivered their tables. Furthermore, customers could personalize their dishes and save their preferences for their next visits.

Panera invested more than $42 million into the implementation of the program with the goal to roll it out to all their restaurants over the next three years. Not only they were able to attract more customers and fend off the increasing competition, but they were able to reinvent the dining experience by transforming the brand into a major technology organization.

Panera was not afraid to challenge the established practices in the fast, casual, and quick-service restaurant industry. Today, it has become the global reference on how technology can empower any retail or food out-of-home business.

Supports
Cola Life is a case of a frugal innovation without incorporating any high-tech elements into the final solution. Simon Berry, an aid worker and social entrepreneur, spent many years helping to distribute medicines to local and underdeveloped communities in Zambia, Africa. During this period, he

realized that the second-biggest cause of child mortality was diarrhea—something apparently simple to prevent. You only need salt and water, what is called ORS in medical terms (oral rehydration salts).

Rather than investing in expensive and new distribution networks, he thought of taking advantage of an existing one, the Coca-Cola distribution system, to deliver life-saving medicines. In some corners of the world, it is sometimes easier to have Coke bottles than clean water. So the simple yet extraordinary solution was to reinvent distribution. Berry created a wedge-shaped package that fit in the spaces between the bottle necks and put the medicines inside it. He named it the AIRPod, a clever and life-saving solution that didn't gain enough attention to get it off the ground. But years later, in April 2008, he decided to give it another shot. At that time, Facebook had already become an influential platform and a new technology to spread the word about this AIRPod solution. The reinvention gained attention on Facebook, and afterward it got noticed by the BBC and then by Coca-Cola. Eventually, Cola Life began collaborating with Coca-Cola's local African operations and could start its first program. Now Cola Life is exploring new packaging shapes in which to store other medicines and water disinfectants.

The product itself didn't integrate any new technology; however, it was thanks to a new digital platform like Facebook that it was able to get the needed attention to bring the project to reality. Technology had a supporting role in the process. ***Think of technology as an essential support to reinvent.***

REINVENTION CAUSES VALUE MIGRATION

Always challenge the old ways.

—HOWARD SCHULTZ, CHAIRMAN AND
CHIEF EXECUTIVE OFFICER OF STARBUCKS

One of the empirical facts about business strategy is that reinventions cause value migration. It has happened throughout the history of business, and it will continue to happen in the future.

In the entertainment industry, value migrated away from TV networks, which broadcasted series, movies, and programs at specific times of the day, to an on-demand content model dominated by YouTube, Netflix, Apple, and Amazon. In the hospitality industry, value migrated away from travel agencies toward do-it-yourself websites where you can now compare hotels, see other customers' reviews, and directly book online through sites like TripAdvisor.

And the same happened with one of the most popular products in the world: coffee. After United States had recovered from the 1982 recession, consumer demand gradually began to soar, especially driving up sales of premium goods. Coffee manufacturers considered it a huge opportunity for the canned coffee category, which had been stagnant throughout the '80s. At that time, it was the only source of growth they could attempt in a market where price competition was ferocious.

So based on that trend, brands started to add premium coffees to their current product portfolios. Folger's coffee launched Gourmet Supreme, and Maxwell House launched Private Collection. They both failed. Those launches didn't move the market share as expected. So they concluded that people were not willing to pay for premium coffees. Meanwhile, as the marketing executives of those brands were sitting in their offices discussing their next price reduction and coupon wave, several companies started to brew a new alternative to cope with the demand for premium coffee. There were new coffee shops that offered customized and fresh-roasted coffee combinations with Italian names such as the caramel macchiato venti. Peets Coffee & Tea, Coffee Bean & Tea Leaf, and Starbucks are the most significant representatives in that category.

The value in the coffee category was moving from a functional and straightforward beverage to a personalized delicacy experience you could enjoy at home. However, Folger's or Maxwell House didn't even move or make any decision based on those new leaders.

Were those coffeehouses even on their radar screens? Of course not. As Theodore Levitt, Harvard marketing professor and author, coined, they had "marketing myopia" or "product provincialism," which means that radically new products are not perceived as being part of an existing business category; they are seen as something foreign and unrelated. Incumbents didn't see themselves as being in the coffee business; they saw themselves in the canned coffee business with products sold on supermarkets shelves. Because Starbucks was not on the supermarket shelves, competing side by side with Folger's and Maxwell House, it was not considered a competitor.

Consequently, these companies missed out on the biggest source of growth in the coffee business in recent history.

Brands compete to deliver value to the consumer. So think of alternative ways and categories to deliver value to the consumer.

Challenge the current value proposition that incumbents are offering to consumers.

THE FOUR PARTICIPANTS IN REINVENTION

There are four players who participate in the reinvention process: pioneers, innovators, imovators, and clones. Each group contributes to reinvention in a different way. Which group do you want to belong to?

Pioneers

The Scottish scientist Alexander Fleming was a pioneer. Dr. Fleming is credited with having discovered penicillin in 1928. Fleming recognized the potential of penicillin but stopped studying it in 1931. He couldn't make it last in the human body. It took a team of Oxford scientists led by the Australian Howard Florey (the reinventors) to mass produce penicillin as a drug. Australia was the first country where penicillin became available to the whole population.[11]

Pioneering does not imply that the market adopts the product. A pioneer is an inventor, not necessarily the marketer or businessman. A pioneer normally sticks with a product for months or even dozens of years until he or she finds a valid way of getting value out of it and sees some potential to commercialize it. It is a long process that takes enormous resources, which is why such pioneers are very rarely able to complete their work. It is not until a reinventor picks up the work with fresh eyes that it can be successfully launched into the mainstream market.

Reinventors

Reinventors are the ones who introduce a new and unique product that the market adopts successfully. This idea of mainstream public adoption is what separates innovators from pure pioneers. Given that innovation is an ongoing evolution, it is better we call them reinventors because they make things evolve in a new and unique way. They never start from scratch.

For instance, White Castle was a fast-food pioneer, but McDonald's became the reinventor. White Castle was acclaimed as the first hamburger fast-food chain when, in 1916, Walter Anderson opened his first burger stand in Wichita, Kansas, and then in 1921 opened his first restaurant under the White Castle brand with his new partner, E. W. Ingram.

White Castle defined the foundations of the fast-food industry in the early '30s, ten years before McDonald's created its first restaurant. The company was an invention machine. It became the first fast-food restaurant to advertise in the newspaper, offering a "five-hamburgers-for-a-dime" coupon, and it was the one that introduced the frozen beef patty with holes. This way they could improve the cooking quality and safety of food and at the same time increase the speed of service.

Despite these facts, who is credited for those inventions and for bringing those ideas to the mass market? McDonald's, now one of the most recognized brands in the world.

Certainly, White Castle was considered an innovator during its first fifteen years. However, it is only with enough time and perspective that we can put the right tags on each of the participants.

Reinventors take advantage of past experimentation and progress made by their precedents, the pioneers, to launch their solutions in a relatively short period of time, limiting the amount invested in the project. However, there is a close wave of competitors that are already in the market, and thanks to their operational flexibility, they are able to imitate a key part of a reinvented product. Those are the imovators.

Imovators

In 2010, there was a memo that got a high level of attention among the employees of a top mobile manufacturer. Without reservation, it was written, "Let's make something like the iPhone." In other words, the chief executive of the company, J. K. Shin, was inviting employees to copy the iPhone. Can you imagine which brand I am talking about? Samsung, a company that is known for being a successful imovator.

An imovator basically imitates in areas where the company is weak and innovates where the company has a clear advantage. So Samsung imitated the user interface of the iPhone and innovated by creating bigger screens with more powerful speakers and higher-resolution cameras. Samsung's ability to produce big displays, memory, and other high-tech features gives it a significant advantage.

This is the imovator strategy. It waits until a brand has established something new, and within a short time, it comes out with a better version to try to lead an entire industry. IBM became an imovator with the personal computer. The idea was Apple's. But within just two years, it was able to take over Apple's leadership position in the personal-computer field. It may not seem a very original strategy, but as I have been mentioning throughout the book, every new product is based on previous technologies and designs. This was also Steve Jobs's starting point when he decided to follow the Xerox user interface to create Apple's first personal computer.

The downside is that when the market leader runs out of new, unique, and valuable features, their imitators will also follow them down the same path. When there is such high dependence between the reinventor and the imovator, that is when a market such as the mobile-phone one starts to suffer, especially with reduced margins and EBITDA (earnings before interest, taxes, depreciation, and amortization). Most imitators find that the only way to make their products more competitive is to push down prices when they have nothing significantly valuable to add to their offerings.

Clones
There is one last set of competitors that can threaten reinventors and even imovators: the clones. Clones are organizations that replicate the exact same offering as the reinventors. They

normally launch that offering in markets where the reinventors have not arrived or try to occupy a lower-end part of their market as a way of stealing shares.

In today's world, reinventors and pioneers are praised, and imovators and clones are disregarded. But what is clear is that all of these different players will always exist, and they will continue to fight against each other as long as the business opportunity is big.

Furthermore, as communication is more global and connected, the stories and business cases of successful new companies are immediately available to anyone. For that reason, we live in an age of imitation. It is a given that companies that will try to copy an original and successful business model. Clones have great incentives. First, a clone avoids many of the mistakes faced by the pioneer or innovator. Second, there is no cost to educate consumers about a new category and persuade them that it is worth its value. Third, they have the chance to improve the innovator´s product and focus on the features that drive demand from day one.

The Groupon business model has probably been one of the most cloned in recent start-up history. The business was based on a "deal-of-the-day" website that offered discounted gift cards to users. Groupon's first deal was "buy two pizzas for the price of one," and twenty people bought the deal. Not only were they giving an offer to customers, but they were also satisfying vendors. Each vendor would be able to gain incremental business. So it was a win-win situation for all.

In less than one year, clones started to appear all over the world, imitating their business model, product offerings, pricing structure, and even their online advertising strategy. Today, it is estimated that there are more than five hundred Groupon clones on a global scale and over one hundred in the United States alone. Since its origins, Groupon has remained the global leader of this new deal of the day that they created in 2008. However, many small players have progressively conquered niche segments within the category and conquered countries where Groupon could not arrive on time or did not have enough resources to develop. Some of these companies were acquired to gain the control back, but others still have a leadership position in other countries, like Groupalia in the Spanish market.

The clones enjoy a free-ride advantage because they can follow the footsteps that the leader has gotten right. They will be able to get more financing opportunities and consequently more resources to invest (talent, expansion, or advertising) given that venture capitalists will see that the business model is already proven. Apparently that would reduce the risk of failure because a clone will only copy successful strategies from category leaders, but risk is always present.

Risk only shifts from the risk of uncertainty by being the pioneer or innovator to other critical areas: Will a clone survive a market flooded with more clones with the same budget and talent? Will a clone be able to make a business model work in another country? Will a clone be able to earn credibility and compete against the leader?

Imitation is more abundant than innovation and is a path more frequently chosen to achieve business growth and profits, a claim that was first made more than twenty-five years ago by Theodore Levitt, the noted Harvard professor.[12] For this reason, the reinventor must elaborate and implement a series of strategies to sustain its position in the long term, especially with the arrival of clones (like in the following case).

Learn from the pioneers. Protect your position against clones and imovators.

THE EXTRATERRESTRIAL CRASH

What is dangerous is not to evolve.

—*JEFF BEZOS, FOUNDER AND CHIEF EXECUTIVE OFFICER OF AMAZON.COM*

The home video-game industry, which began with the launch of the arcade game Pong from Atari, Inc. in 1971, had peaked in 1982 to $2 billion in revenue. However, by 1985 the number fell to around $100 million. Some people may call it "Atari shock," but it was more a full industry crash.

What happened? Well, something very related to Lasky's adventure and to the dot-com crash in 2001. The market was saturated with new gaming consoles: Atari, Bally Astrocade, ColecoVision, Emercion Arcadia, Fairchild Channel F, Magnavox Odyssey, and Mattel Intellivision, just to mention a few. Each gaming console had its own platform and its own library of games, and some consoles also had large third-party libraries that were built only for that specific console. Furthermore, hundreds of game publishers appeared, launching low-quality games to the market and mostly offering games that were copying the original versions with just minuscule differences. Most stores didn't have enough space to display all games and consoles. All in all, consumers just lost confidence in this market, and that led to a steep decline that lasted two years until 1985.

The collapse of the industry together with the long production cycle of games resulted in gigantic inventory levels. One of the most iconic inventory nightmares was associated with the game ET: The Extraterrestrial, which was not able to sell as expected, and finally they had to dump six million cartridges into a landfill. Recently, a production company initiated a dig into the landfill to discover what has been one of the biggest secrets in the gaming industry in history.

New and growing categories will attract competitors. They will try to clone your original offering; it is a fact. And they will probably try to compete on price with lower-quality versions of the original product and consequently potentially destroy the whole category like what happened in the previous case. So, as a reinventor, if you want keep owning the category you created, you will need to plan accordingly, which is the subject I will cover in the next chapters. Just being the creator of a growing category is not going to be synonymous with success.

Predict what's next, and know when to evolve—or competitors will catch you.

INVENT YOUR ENEMY FROM THE START

Work like there is someone working twenty-four hours a day to take it away from you.

—MARK CUBAN, BUSINESSMAN, INVESTOR, AND
OWNER OF THE NBA's DALLAS MAVERICKS

Think that somewhere in the world at this same moment, one entrepreneur will be creating a product or service like yours; it could even be in the same country or city. And now also think that company will use the same strategy as you are planning to implement. Why do I suggest inventing your enemy? Because this is, in fact, what is happening, even though you are still not aware of it.

Taking this into account, rethink your business strategy, and plan for imitation strategies. At the end of the day, if no company clones your business model or imitates your marketing strategy, it is because the opportunity you are going after is not as profitable as you expected. And even in those cases, imitators will appear because they will be following the same wrong business opportunity.

Only the paranoid survive.

HOW TO DETER IMITATION AND DEFEND AGAINST IMITATORS

The name of the game is not only how to defend against imitators with short-term tactical marketing campaigns but, more importantly, how to deter imitation strategies in the medium and long terms. There are two set of enemies.

Short Term: Clones

Small companies with a high operational flexibility and speed to market are usually the first ones to imitate your company. These are companies that are focused on replicating the proven winning formula, consequently giving them focus on where to invest production and marketing resources. Some of these imitators will copy and paste your business model, creating a clone.

So to survive the "attack of the clones," there are three key strategies:

1. The speed of growth, which does not mean to launch directly to the mass market; it still requires a grassroots approach to gain traction, credibility, and enthusiasm community by community.
2. The ability to create a brand that is strongly associated with the new category. In the minds of the consumers, the rest of the brands will just be a copy with dubious credibility and with an unauthentic image.
3. Anticipating which are the most attractive segments for a new entrant and preparing accordingly. As a marketer, you know that a new entrant will clone your business model; however one can do so at many different levels:

Geography: In which market do they want to compete? Side by side in a local market or in a new country? You will probably face both situations at the same time. So the brand needs to stay focused, executing the planned geographic expansion strategy. If you envision growing city by city, don't get distracted by a new competitor serving a different city.

Target market: Will the new entrant target the same customers, or will it look for a different sociodemographic and different lifestyle segment?

Product value: Some clones will position themselves at the same price level; however it is more frequent that the new entrants will start to occupy the premium or value segment within the category your brand has created. As the category leader, you can either cede the low end of the market to new competitors or reduce their opportunity by introducing a low-end offer in order to share that part of the market with them. It can reduce margins in the short run, but it could be a way of planning to fight them from the beginning.

Long Term: Incumbents

Large and established multinationals on the other side do not tend to rush to enter a new market. Their priority is to be certain of the success of the new category before investing resources there. They have ways of getting growth from a new category:

* Acquiring overperforming companies from a new category.

* Launching their own solution but with one hundred times more advertising, distribution, and operations support than the category leader.

Is this, however, the winning formula? Not always. In some cases, a company like Coca-Cola can buy the category leader of vitamin waters by acquiring the brand Vitamin Water. In some other cases, Coca-Cola is still chasing the category leader in energy drinks (Red Bull) with its own version (Burn) and also cutting the distance by becoming a partner of the second-largest player in the category, Monster.

So to outcompete existing brands in the market, the key is to plan for the long term by:

1. Building a core advantage: create an offering that cannot be copied operationally.
2. Not overprotecting: invest in continuous innovation.

BUILD A CORE ADVANTAGE

*You are not your idea, and if you identify
too closely with your ideas, you will take
offense when they are challenged.*

—ED CATMULL, PRESIDENT OF PIXAR ANIMATION
STUDIOS AND WALT DISNEY STUDIOS

Create a business that cannot be copied by existing big players at an operational level. Copying a business by communicating that it is the same is easy for any competitor, especially if it has the resources to do so.

Competitors can easily build a new communication strategy replicating your company's look and feel. However, it would be much more difficult for them to imitate a business model that is linked with a unique set of operations. That is why it is so critically important that the new solution you create resides at the core of your organization. By that, I mean that your operations must also visually communicate it to the consumer.

Take Subway as an example. Subway is perceived as a healthier place to eat a sandwich worldwide when compared to the traditional fast-food chains; it has become the owner of this category. This has been the consequence of focusing their efforts on the "eat fresh" positioning as well of having operations supporting their words.

Subway operations are built around the value of freshness. There are no fryers in the restaurants, you can see the fresh ingredients all lined up, and you can even select what you want. McDonald's could try to bring their own sub sandwiches to the market, but they would never be able to offer an environment without fryers or where you can see how the staff creates your sandwich. So you have to make those operational differences visible to the customer. You have to support your positioning with a real and authentic solution. Develop a solution that resides at the core, not just on a product feature or a tagline, and keep the solution fresh over time.

As an American businessman, an investor, and the owner of the NBA's Dallas Mavericks, Mark Cuban says, "To think that whoever it is you are competing with, they are just going to let you come in and take their business, obviously that is naïve, and I think most people don't recognize that."[13] Any core advantage will need to evolve and be reinvented, including Subway's in order to protect the fresh and personalized food subcategory that the brand successfully created decades ago. Ultimately, "fresh" has evolved to mean something very different to consumers today, and nowadays every brand is jumping on the personalized-food-made-in-front-of-you bandwagon, making it a more crowded and undifferentiated territory.

It won't be enough to match the fresh claims from every other brand in the food out-of-home market such as clean labeling and local sourcing. Subway will need to bring unique and brave innovation that gives brand credibility, relevancy, and energy to take their core equity—freshness—to the next level. Only by doing so will Subway be able to set the brand apart and put it into a new space, back as a leader of the fresh category again (this is something I cover in more detail in the next chapter).

Another way of building a core advantage to defend your brand against imitators is to build a proprietary platform. Nike created the Nike+ platform, Apple created the iTunes platform, and the HD Hero Camera built a series of accessories to mount the video camera on, including countless objects from helmets to surfboards.

It is about shifting away from singular products and toward systems and brand experiences. It is about the connection between the different devices that interact with the consumer.

Reinvent systems and environments that connect consumers to your operations, and keep it fresh over time.

DON'T OVERPROTECT; INVEST IN CONTINUOUS INNOVATION

People can copy what you've done, but they can't copy what you're going to do.

—DENNIS CROWLEY, COFOUNDER AND
EXECUTIVE CHAIRMAN OF FOURSQUARE

Reinventing a category with a new product or service is not the end goal; it is a process that never stops. You need to keep your offer relevant and unique to core customers.

Let's take Atari, the pioneer in video games. Atari was created by the entrepreneur and visionary Nolan Bushnell in 1972 with only $250. Bushnell, also considered the father of video games, was able to make Atari the fastest-growing company in the history of the United States. Not only that, but it had a great influence on some of its earliest employees such as Steve Jobs and Steve Wozniak, the founders of Apple Computer.

It all started with reinventing arcade games. Atari's first product was a coin-operated and very simple arcade game where a player only needed one hand on the joystick to play. New generations would now consider it like a highly rudimentary and archaic tennis game, only consisting of two vertical bars on each side of the screen and one ball, which, at that time, was square. That was the birth of modern video games.

In less than three months, game manufacturers began launching their own Pong-game versions. Even though Bushnell applied for a patent and trademark, Atari didn't get the required legal protection to stop new players from invading the market. By 1974, 100,000 "Pong games" were produced, and only one out of ten was produced by Atari. Nonetheless, Atari generated $3.2 million that year.

Did Atari stop at that point? Atari made $13 million with sales of Pong and other new games in the next three years. Its key to success was to out-innovate the competition. Atari launched one game every month during 1974. Bushnell's fast innovation strategy allowed Atari to defend itself from competitors. Once a competitor launched a copy, Atari responded by launching a new game.[14]

But did Atari stop at that point? Not only did Atari continue launching new games every month, but its next move was even more extreme. Why not bring the arcade game machines to people's living rooms? Why not reinvent the arcade game industry?

So in 1975, Atari created a new category, home video games. It designed the first gaming machine ever that used the TV set as the screen. Atari sold 150,000 units in the 1975 Christmas season,[15] and its sales nearly hit $40 million.[16]

Again, with this level of success came the "jackals," as Bushnell used to call imitators. Seventy-five companies planned to launch lookalike home tennis video games in 1976.

Don't be afraid to replace yourself. Successful innovators know when it's time to replace some of their current products before a competitor beats them. Be open to risks, and constantly ask yourself how you would out-innovate and outperform yourself.

Aim for a constant mark of quality and newness rather than being a one-hit wonder.

DAVID VERSUS GOLIATH

First they ignore you, then they laugh at you, then they fight you, then you win.

—Mahatma Gandhi

This is pretty much the process every reinvention faces. Getting ignored or laughed at doesn't harm a new product. On the contrary, it is a good thing to be underestimated. However, when incumbents decide to fight, that's when a brand needs to be prepared big time. Therefore, winning is not a given in this case.

Sometimes successful innovations are so radically different that they don't fit into the current way of doing things. So a very frequent scenario is to see big industry leaders coming together to stop those innovations. Lawyers, lobbies…you name it. They will do anything in their power to ensure that the new players, those who pose a threat, are rejected by the current system.

When the start-ups Uber, Lyft, Sidecar, and InstantCab (rebranded as Summon) reinvented the taxi industry, they were accused of violating several California laws because they used "community drivers" or non-cab drivers without a specific permission to conduct business on airport property. The case quickly extended to other cities like New York.

Do you like chocolate? British brewers didn't like it in 1763. At that time, hot chocolate began to grow as a very popular beverage until the point when they began considering it as a threat and started thinking that chocolate drinks would directly steal beer sales. So breweries got together to try to establish a law to limit chocolate production.

Would you like to have a caffeine-free cola? When the soft drink manufacturer Canada Dry launched Sport, the first cola drink without caffeine, in 1967, Coca-Cola felt so threatened that it initiated legal action and influenced the FDA (US Food and Drug Administration) to rule that the new beverage was illegally labeled before Sport even reached national distribution. Coca-Cola and the FDA reasoned that any cola drink should contain caffeine because its main ingredient comes from the kola nut, a fruit with high caffeine content. Otherwise, it could not be labeled as a cola drink.[17]

Coca-Cola won the battle, and Canada Dry had to remove its product from the stores. However, that could not stop the avalanche of companies introducing caffeine-free colas in the following years. Why weren't those new brands prosecuted? Because at that time, even the government was recommending avoiding high doses of caffeine.

In this case, Canada Dry paid the highest price for being the pioneer. The problem was that Canada Dry didn't follow rule number one: the core advantage has to be inside the core of a company. It was fairly easy for Coke to develop its own caffeine-free version. It was not a core innovation; it was just a new product feature.

Incumbents will try any sort of unfair tactics to get your business out of the market. It happened in the past, it happens now, and it will continue to happen in the future. Even in the early 1880s, Thomas Alva Edison began one of the most extreme campaigns in modern history to discredit his main rivals, the Serbian engineer Nicola Tesla and the American entrepreneur John Westinghouse. Edison, who was promoting his power plants that used direct current (DC), began a negative publicity campaign to demonstrate how dangerous it would be to adopt his competitors' model, the power plants that used alternative current (AC).

The price? Enough to light up New York City. Edison claimed that his system had less voltage but was far more secure, given the fact that electric cables were buried underground. However, according to Edison, Westinghouse's AC system used a higher voltage to distribute electricity, making it a threat to the public. At first, Edison tried to have legislation on his side to limit the power of transmission voltages, but he failed. So he hired an external engineer called Harold P. Brown to influence people in his favor. Brown used Westinghouse's alternating current to electrocute stray dogs. Then he used goats and even horses. Finally, to show what could happen to humans, he persuaded New York State that AC could be used to execute condemned prisoners. In 1890, the electric chair was born.

Despite Edison's efforts, he failed to stop the development of Westinghouse's electric system, and he even failed to popularize the phrase "to be Westinghoused," referring to the electric-chair execution.

This might be an extreme case of discrediting a competitor, but be certain that it will happen to any company that poses a threat to the status quo such as Uber with the cab association or Airbnb with the hotel industry.

If your brand is under attack, it is because you are probably doing something right.

Part 2

BUILD

Don't spend so much time trying to choose the perfect opportunity that you miss the right opportunity.

—MICHAEL DELL, FOUNDER AND CHIEF EXECUTIVE OFFICER OF DELL INC.

As a marketing executive, when you identify an interesting business idea, the first thing you normally do is comb the market and check if there is something similar around. You type the key words into Google, and you see that it has already been done. Someone has already built a similar business, and that company has been operating for a significant amount of time.

Then you question, "If the idea has already been done, why hasn't it worked?" Is it because the idea didn't resonate with today's consumers? Or because the company failed in the implementation? Thinking about it is a fair thing to do. However, creating a business is not just about having a great idea. Businesses are more complex than that, and an idea is just a small part of the equation. There were more than three hundred online video sites before YouTube launched its business. What YouTube did differently was to create a simple video-sharing platform where people could easily embed videos throughout the web and social media sites.

Another example from the online world is the success of Yelp, the online review site. In 2005, when Yelp began its operations, there were hundreds of sites already reviewing restaurants and other local businesses. By that time, it was already an old business model with a market leader, Citysearch, struggling to keep its position and financial viability. What Yelp did differently than the other sites is to focus on attracting a small community of motivated reviewers to share authentic and valuable opinions. Yelp didn't pay reviewers to comment on their experiences. Instead, Yelp motivated them by making sure that their reviews were seen and valued by consumers. Something more scalable and that produced higher added value from users was the Yelp difference.

Don't overthink the idea phase. Start building and experimenting in order to validate the initial idea. At the end of the day, you need to examine if you can transform that idea into a product, if consumers will buy it and stick with it, and if you will be able to sustain it over the years by generating a profit.

2.1. EXPERIMENT

*Waiting for perfect is never as
smart as making progress.*

—SETH GODIN, ENTREPRENEUR, BEST-
SELLING AUTHOR, AND PUBLIC SPEAKER

It is far easier to figure out if a product works and is positively received by consumers than to spend too much time predicting its success. You don't want to build a mathematical success that, at the end of the day, will become a marketing and innovation failure.

Any significant successful innovation began as an experiment and was tested on a small scale to discover its market potential. As Andrew Grove, chairman of Intel Corporation, puts it, "Innovation does not come in the form of a figurative light bulb going on. It comes through experimentation."[18]

MATHEMATICAL SUCCESSES, MARKETING FAILURES

In the marketing industry, we tend to overrate the importance of creating long-term and formalized marketing plans. We tend to create marketing plans that are mathematical successes, but in reality they are marketing failures. You can plan a detailed outline of the goals, marketing investment, media planning, and new product launches; however, two things could happen. First, the marketing strategy or the marketing mix might not be right. Second, an existing competitor could launch an aggressive promotion, or a new player could enter the market with a new and stronger offering.

Some people call these rare and unexpected events "the black swan." However, they are never rare because they will certainly happen. Sooner or later your company will be challenged by a black swan, and if you don't consider these events, your company will be washed away from the market.

Marketing plans as we know them are obsolete. So to be highly competitive in a market, a company must be organized and prepared to shift its direction and have a margin of maneuverability in case the marketing strategy or marketing mix is not effective in the market.

The solution to this problem is experimentation. Exploit different channels, customers, and products. Then stick with the winning formula. Succeeding with innovations involves experimentation, and experimentation involves failures. Now, errors are beneficial as long as you meet two criteria. First, you have to fail cheap and fast. Second, you have to fix the problem fast. A nonperforming experimental strategy or marketing mix cannot be in the market too long; you don't want an experiment to burn through all of your company's cash.

A marketing plan should be flexible enough to take into account the failures and lessons from the experimentation phase.

Everyone has a plan till they
get punched in the mouth.

—*MIKE TYSON, AMERICAN*
FORMER PROFESSIONAL BOXER

EXPERIMENT CHEAP AND FAST

Innocent is a smoothies company initiated by a group of young people living in London; they did not have much time to cook or to go to the gym, and they had lots of pizza and junk food in their daily food habits until they realized that they had to change their lifestyles to healthier ones. So their solution was fruit smoothies ready to drink—natural fruit crushed up and put into bottles that busy people can drink during the day in the office, at home, or on the go.

As you might imagine, they had scarce marketing resources to launch their product, so they had to spend it wisely. Before investing their own money in developing the product, they wanted to be certain that the product would be a hit. So they decided to do some smoothies trials at music festivals. They could have opted to develop a traditional questionnaire and ask people about their age, gender, and interests, how much they liked the taste from 1 to 5, and so on. Instead, they came up with a more engaging and effective approach. They used the bins as a consumer satisfaction measure. They placed two bins side by side and put up a sign on top that read, "Should we give up our jobs to make these smoothies?" They had a yes sign on top of one bin and a no on top of the other bin. At the end of the day, the yes bin was completely full, and the "bin test," as they called it, was their first milestone to success.

Testing is important, but it can also cost thousands of dollars that you might not have, plus you can get sidetracked and overloaded with unnecessary information. Ask a clear and actionable question like they did, which basically was "Should we take this project to the next level and risk our jobs?" It is simple and engaging because they put the decision in consumers' hands.

Build your own testing bin, and proof your concept.

REBELS OF EXPERIMENTATION

Companies should always be in a test-and-learn mode, both at their birth stage and mature stage. Finding the optimal business model, strategy, and marketing mix is not a linear process; it always comes after iterative experimentation. All the components of the marketing mix have to be tested and adjusted: communication (including the messaging, channels, framing), customer segment, price, and distribution channels. You have to find out the optimal marketing mix fast until results follow. Keep rearranging it until you feel it snap into place.

Twitter, for instance, was born in 2007 at the South-by-Southwest conference when they created a new platform to distribute text messages to multiple users. Today, Twitter has more than 650 million active users, and every second there are 9,100 tweets sent; it only takes five days to get to one billion tweets. Every single industry knows about the power of Twitter. It has helped a president get to the White House, it has built brands, and it has also destroyed reputations and businesses. Its impact is undeniable. And it all began with a fast and low-cost experiment to challenge how traditional text messages were being used. It challenged the established status quo.

Think about the Facebook experiment. What were you doing in October 2003? At that time, a Harvard student compiled hundreds of ID photos of his university fellows and created a website so that people could vote if those people were hot or not. It was a copy of a website highly popular among college students, Hot or Not, where people were rated based on their physical attractiveness. The site lived for three days and disappeared. You could think this had no impact on our daily lives, but in fact that was Mark Zuckerberg's experiment, where he saw the potential of social media for college students, an interest that later on proved to be shared by millions of people from all over the world.

It all begins with a low-cost and rapid-fire experiment.

PIVOTING

Failure is not the opposite of success,
but a stepping stone to success.

—*ARIANNA HUFFINGTON, COFOUNDER AND*
EDITOR-IN-CHIEF OF THE HUFFINGTON POST

Beware of throwing an idea to the bin or giving up your business unless you have tried pivoting it. Rarely will the initial business idea be the one that will get the most traction in the market.

Pivoting is a term that has gotten popular these last few years, especially when Eric Ries described it in his book *The Lean Startup* in 2011. However, this is not a new concept. Andrew Grove already described and published it in his book *Only the Paranoid Survive* in 1996.

Rarely does a company find success and stick with the first product it launches and its first marketing strategy. In most cases, products need to be rebuilt, customer targets need to be shifted, and distribution channels need to be reconsidered in order to find the optimal marketing mix that captures people's interest in the market. That is what pivoting is for.

I tend to use the example of pivoting in basketball, which consists of stepping with one foot while keeping the other foot at its point of contact with the floor. It involves maintaining certain parts of the company strategy as fixed and which work as an axis and then changing the rest to turn around a situation.

Pivoting is a survival tool for any new venture. The New York Statue of Liberty that we all know would not be there if the Egyptians had dismissed its initial version, which had to decorate the Suez Canal entry in the nineteenth century.

The French artist Frédéric Auguste Bartholdi initially designed the statue as an homage to the Egyptian progress. He initially proposed to sketch a colossal robed farmer holding a torch that would serve as a lighthouse. It was intended to symbolize the industrial revolution that the country was living through, especially after the opening of the Suez Canal in 1869. However, Bartholdi soon found out that he would not be able to proceed with his project.

But the artist came up with an alternative market for his statue after traveling several times to the United States. He spotted a small island—Bedloe's Island—on his way to New York, which everyone would interpret as the entrance to the land of freedom and democracy. But first he had to adapt his design to make it relevant for the new market. Instead of the veil that covered the statue's head, he substituted it for a diadem. He changed the torch from her left hand to her right. And because she now had nothing in her left hand, he added a tablet, which was inscribed with the date of the American Declaration of Independence, July IV MDCCLXXVI. To add a final touch, he put a broken chain on the feet of the statue. He sold his project to the French government as a great gift to commemorate the perseverance of freedom and democracy in the United States and to honor the work of the late president Abraham Lincoln. Bartholdi was able to successfully pivot his original design and make it relevant for the American market.

A company will probably have to go through several pivots before succeeding in the market. So it is also useful to be aware of the most frequent types of pivots and how different companies succeeded by implementing them.

Zoom In

Zooming in is about rebuilding a company around a specific product feature that presents an unexpected growth potential.

In 2002, a start-up called Ludicorp was created by Caterina Flake, Stewart Buttefield, and Jason Classon. Ludicorp launched a multiplayer online game called Game Neverending, where users could interact with real-time instant messaging. In 2004, the founders added a photo-sharing capability within the messaging service in the game, a feature that gained popularity among users, even surpassing the game's popularity. So after the founding team identified the success of that product feature, they created a photo-sharing community called Flickr. The company was so successful that in March 2005, it was acquired by Yahoo.

Zoom Out

Zooming out is about broadening the initial value proposition to users. YouTube started as a way of sharing videos; however, it evolved as an online and social TV channel, with YouTube producers (partners) earning money from the advertising that the company puts before watching the video and around YouTube partners' sites. YouTube zoomed out from its initial proposition of sharing videos between users to creating an online TV network and community.

Customer Segment Pivot

The first product you have launched could have built a solid customer baseline for your business. However, the opportunities of a new technology combined with unsatisfying financial results could allow you to rethink your original product while maintaining your customer baseline. At the end of the day, pivoting is about moving your business to a more successful market position by taking advantage of a key asset—in this case, your acquired customers.

In February 2010, the serial entrepreneur Jason Goldberg and interior designer Bradford Shellhammer founded Fabulis. com, a social networking site targeted toward the gay community that tried to capture a bite of the Facebook, Yelp, and Groupon market share. Its model lacked clarity, and that translated into a low user base (only 175,000 one year after) and unsatisfactory financial results. So Fabulis.com transformed into a flash sales site called Fab.com, in what is known in Silicon Valley as one of the most successful pivots of the decade.

However, they did not start from scratch. For more than a year and a half, they had acquired a small fan base that they could use, a pivotal point worth taking advantage of. The new site, Fab.com, sold designer housewares, accessories, clothing, and jewelry. Even though it was not specifically targeted at a gay audience, it clearly evoked interest from their previous user base. In 2012, seven months after the pivot, the site achieved a milestone of more than two million users and grew from three employees to one hundred.

Pivoting should be the practice of capitalizing on what a new business has accomplished during its first stages in the market. In this case, Fab.com turned around the business, taking advantage of the user base they had built throughout its first stage.

Plan for several possible futures.

THE DANGERS OF EXPERIMENTING

Experimentation is part of the DNA of companies that aspire to reinvent a category, but it also has one downside. Experimentation could make your organization lose focus and dilute a marketing budget and employees' valuable time with too many side projects. That is why experimentation requires focus.

So how do you filter experimentation? What is worth testing, and what is not worth the investment of time, money, and resources?

Experimentation should be focused on three things. First, it should be focused on building upon the brand's vision. Not only does it need to identify a new category that is aligned with the brand, but it also needs to enhance a brand's purpose and equity. Second, experimentation needs to be focused on delivering a set of financial expectations that each company needs to define based on its goals and industry. Third, it is about finding the optimal strategy and marketing mix: product, message, target, price, promotions, and operations that lead to brand relevance, energy, and visibility. Marketing teams need to test and experiment in order to find the right balance of those elements.

Experiment with a clear purpose and expectations.

2.2. START SMALL-BUT DO START

Nothing we design or make ever really works...Everything we design and make is an improvisation, a lash-up, something inept and provisional.

—David William Pye, professor of furniture design at The Royal College of Art

Projects tend to seem big at the beginning. So the majority of people don't even begin working on their ideas just because it seems so unmanageable and intimidating. You have to start small to get started. Using your hands not only allows you to get a deep understanding of your business and of creating unique products, but it also allows you to build something quick and cheap.

In 1898, a young inventor named H. Cecil Booth attended an exhibition at the London Empire Music Hall. There, an American designer was showcasing his new dust-removing machine. It was one of the first attempts to create the modern vacuum cleaner. However, the machine worked the other way around from what we are used to now. There was a metal box with a compressed air compartment on top that blew the dust from the carpet in a way that all the dust spread all over the room. Clearly the concept of blowing down the dust was not thought of right from the beginning.

But this inspired H. Cecil Booth to try a different approach. Why not suck up the dust instead? So he began testing his new concept straight away. Instead of spending weeks or even months developing his first prototype, he invented the modern vacuum machine with two basic tools: his mouth and a handkerchief. Frugal innovation in its purest state. He opened his mouth, put a filter inside, and leaned down to suck up a seat plush. Booth immediately choked, but he realized that the air power should go upward instead of downward to truly capture the dust instead of spreading it. The key would be to make a filter that trapped dust and let air pass through.

He patented the suction cleaner in 1901. Months after his invention, he was already in business vacuuming theaters and even the carpet in Westminster Abbey for the coronation of Edward VII. And it all started with the simplest prototype one can imagine: his mouth and a handkerchief.

Nike's first product started as a sports shoe with an innovative and unique rubber sole. The first prototype was built with the most basic tools you can imagine, a new product especially useful for the track at the University of Oregon, which had been recently changed to an artificial surface. Phil Knight and Bill Bowerman, track-and-field coaches and Nike's cofounders, wanted to create a sole without metal spikes and made from a new material that could deliver a high-performance grip.

It was built inside the house of cofounder Phil Knight. The shoe was made from melting latex and cooking it in a waffle maker. Knight even had to wait until his wife went to church to get into the garage and use the waffle iron. The result was a squared pattern that would allow runners to get a tighter grip on the track.

Creating things with your own hands is a common trait in many other successful companies. There are more examples than you can imagine. Before Banana Republic turned their khakis into gold, there was an initial phase where the two founders, Mel and Patricia Ziegler, literally built their first product with their hands. During one trip to Australia, Mel walked into a surplus store in Sydney and picked up a cotton khaki jacket that looked very cool and authentic. On their way back, his wife, Patricia, quickly saw its potential and started to make some improvements. She added leather elbow patches and wooden buttons to turn it more into a safari style rather than military style. Mel wore the jacket everywhere, and people asked him where he had bought it. It was a quick and cheap way to test the interest of people and what they could do as a business. The next step was to repeat the operation on a slightly bigger scale by buying old paratrooper shirts in an Oakland warehouse, modifying them, and then selling them again with their own safari style.

Marc Ecko, founder of the clothing brand Ecko, began his entrepreneurial path in the same way. Marc had a special interest in graffiti, so he decided to start painting T-shirts and wearing them. He began really young, and even in high-school kids would ask, "Where did you get that?" When Marc said he had done it, people started asking for the products. Some weeks he would earn between six and seven hundred dollars in cash. Again, this is the cheapest and quickest way to test the interest in your product.

As entrepreneurs, we often tend to start executing the idea three or four steps too far from where we should. It is easy to fall into the trap of starting to build a business that is way too big for our investment capacity. We also realize that it will take months before we will have the finished product, and we can also lose time by overthinking about the operation complexities that we will face during the first years. However, if you start up in the most frugal way, suddenly you realize that the project you want to create is more manageable in terms of costs. You can even start with your own hands, and if you don't know how, you can learn.

You can start by "waffling" your shoes or by spray painting your jacket, but do start.

BUILD IT FAST

There is a saying in Silicon Valley: "If you're not embarrassed by your first version of the product you've launched, you've launched too late." It is a phrase that originated from Reid Hoffman, founder of LinkedIn.

Subway, the restaurant chain with the most number of outlets in the world (even surpassing McDonalds), began from a conversation between Fred DeLuca and with his family friend Pete Buck at a casual barbeque in July 1965. DeLuca was hoping that Buck would give him a loan to pay back his studies after graduation, but instead he proposed a better idea: building a sandwich business. Buck read an article about Mike's Submarine Sandwich, a sandwich chain founded by Michael Davis that had opened thirty-two stores in ten years. This was a business story that became Subway's inspiration and goal at the same time. Only one month later, in August 1965, they had already opened their first store.

How did they do it so fast? The same day Pete proposed to Fred to build this business, they spent several hours discussing the menu and prices even before knowing the food and operational costs. The next morning, they began to look for a small store. As soon as they paid the landlord, they began designing the restaurant themselves. They bought a cash register and, with their own hands, built the space to prepare the food as well as the storage area and the counter. DeLuca's mom helped them contact various suppliers who would provide meats, bread, vegetables, cheeses, and drinks. His dad helped him find classified ads in the local newspapers that sold secondhand equipment: a cash register, a refrigeration unit, a commercial sink, a meat slicer, and some shelves to store the products.

Launching your business fast will accelerate the learning curve because, at the end of the day, consumers will be the ones who will define your final product in the market—not your mind and not the time spent overthinking all the details of the business. Don't overthink; just do it. Furthermore, it will give you a competitive advantage with big market players. Giants have a culture of process. New ventures can have a culture of speed. While a big corporation enters a first product evaluation, a small brand has already launched the product. While giants review the first prototype, a small brand has already launched an improved version of your product.

Win on speed.

THE LEAN START-UP

This fast, experimental, and down-to-earth approach is what it is commonly known as the "lean start-up," an approach that relies on validated learning from experimentation, early valuable customer feedback, and iterative product releases to accelerate the product development process.

The term seems as if it was a new concept, especially after several Silicon Valley companies have admitted to having used this approach in their early stages (such as Zappos). In Zappos' case, before launching a full version of its website and stocking itself with expensive shoes, its founder, Nick Swinmurn, created a fast experiment to validate the market. He developed a basic website, took pictures from the inventory of different local shoe stores, and uploaded them online. When someone bought the shoes, he bought them at full price from the local store and delivered them to the customer. Fast, cheap, and actionable.

But we can find other experimentation cases even before the Silicon Valley era. Subbuteo, the table soccer game created by Peter Adolph, also originated from a test. Adolph published an advertisement in the August 1946 issue of *The Boys' Own Paper* magazine. The advert was a test for a product he had not yet created, which means he even advertised the product without an approved patent, which he got later that year.

The product was finally launched in March 1947, six months after the initial ad. There was an unexpected over-load of consumer responses that caught him unprepared and without enough resources to satisfy the demand. So he had to start production from his home with the help of his family and friends—not an easy task considering the shortages after the second World War and their limited experience.

Focus on launching a beta version of the product as soon as you have it ready. This guides us to the next question: when is a product considered good enough to be introduced in a market?

THE MINIMUM LOVABLE PRODUCT

We are aware of how important it is to quickly launch your first product version into the marketplace. Launching early is the best way to get real consumer feedback that is actually valuable rather than overthinking if the market will be interested in it. However, the big question is: how elaborate should a product be in order to launch it?

Here is where the minimum viable product (a.k.a. MVP) comes into the equation. MVP supporters recommend designing the most basic version of the product that solves a consumer problem. This is something every entrepreneur has to define in the first stages of the product development.

You have to take into account whatever tools and market knowledge is available to you at the present time. What you have at a certain moment in time is what you will use to build your product. New technologies or new products from competitors are relevant for the future and for a second version of your product but are certainly irrelevant when you think about a product today.

The problem is that many people take this MVP concept too literally and skimp on the design as well as the scope. Rather than seeing it as a first opportunity to make an impression in the market, especially among influencers, they create a functional product that works but is not worth sharing the news about with others.

What you want is a first product that clearly delivers the new and unique functionality to consumers. Build something they feel enthusiastic about and that they are willing to spread the word about. Build a minimum lovable product (a.k.a. MLP).

Accept a good enough version of your dream product and launch it. There will be plenty of time for refinement later. But make sure it connects with the first influential community of users. In this way, by focusing on the most basic lovable version of the offering and improving the product in a sequential process, you will be able to better optimize the limited budget you will have for product development and promotion.

> *It's better to build something that*
> *a small number of users love than*
> *a large number of users like.*

—*Sam Altman, president of Y Combinator*

THE POWER OF PARTNERSHIPS

Rarely will a recently created company have within the organization the ability to integrate all of the operations that a new product requires at the start. By that I mean from distribution and marketing to manufacturing. Therefore, it is important to team up with same-sized companies that compensate for our lack of resources.

Innocent Drinks started this way. At first, they sold their smoothies from a market at a music festival in London and bought ingredients from a farmer named Jeff, who quickly became involved with the company by helping them make the right choice of fruits and vegetables as well as delivering them to their office. On this experimental stage, they were able to create the smoothies using their own hands and buying from a small supplier.

However, when they expanded their area of influence, they needed to partner up with a larger manufacturing partner. It didn't make sense at this stage to invest in a factory because of the overhead costs and more operational headaches. Manufacturing was definitely not their business. On top of that, at an early stage, a company must possess flexibility to shift products or to add new ingredients to better adjust to consumers' needs. They wouldn't have been able to do it by owning and running their own manufacturing plant. At an early stage, they needed responsiveness. In fact, this allowed them to make many adjustments—for instance, changing from a one-liter plastic bottle to a carton bottle, which otherwise would have cost them millions of pounds.

The same happens in other areas such as advertising and promotion. Imagine you own a small bicycle company for kids, and you are interested in creating events where kids can compete and meet new friends, and at the same time you can create brand awareness highly relevant to the target. Why walk this path alone? The bicycle company could partner with a food company that provides food samples and cover 50 percent of the event cost, while you provide the material, the circuit, and the coordination of the event.

Partnerships can also enhance a brand purpose and raise brand awareness. The salad chain Sweetgreen partnered with the renowned top chef Dan Barber from the farm-to-table Blue Hill restaurant to support the WastED movement, a culture and food movement that aims at reducing food wastage by creating new dishes out of food scraps, which Barber has been a great supporter of from years ago. Who knew there were so many uses for broccoli leaves, kale stems, or roasted bread butts? Toss them in a frittata, use them for vegetable stock, puree them, or shred them into a salad like they did. The WastED, Sweetgreen, and Dan Barber salad got covered by nationwide media, getting millions of dollars' worth of free advertising for their brands.

The power of partnerships is not only strong but is also necessary to compensate for an initial lack of financial resources and knowledge.

The difference between where your brand is and where you want to take it can be narrowed through smart partnerships.

TIMING

Successful reinventors have superb timing. But what determines when to launch a new project?

If you work for a big company, you can have the luxury of watching different trends evolve in the marketplace, analyzing the best fit for the business, and then potentially buying a stake in the new category by acquiring a successful small business.

However, if you are a leading a small brand or a big brand with an entrepreneurial mind-set, the story is quite the opposite. Small brands need to launch their projects when consumers start to adopt new behaviors. It is not obvious to the general public, but a trend is certainly already taking place within a small group of people with shared interests. To capitalize on this requires an informed vision as well as a leap of faith that this trend will grow over time.

Nike, for example, was formed in 1964, when people began to show an interest in practicing sports to keep healthy and in shape. It was a tiny market, so Nike focused on selling their shoes to the professional track athletes. Ten years later, in 1974, Nike was still a relatively small company with revenues of $4.8 million. However, it was in the '70s that the fitness trend and the weekend athletes began to appear, growing the category to billions of dollars in the following years. Nike was there at the right time with the right product. By the early 1990s, Nike soared to the astonishing figure of $3 billion in sales.[19]

Nike was there before the fitness trend exploded. The same thing happened to other reinventors like Nick Goodman, founder of GoPro. In 2002, Goodman had the idea of creating a portable and attachable camera for surfboards and then launched his first product in 2004, one year before the launch of YouTube and the uncontrollable trend of sharing videos on the Internet. When the trend exploded, Goodman was already there with the right product.

Be in the market for when the trend takes off.

ENTERING EARLY

A common question is whether to enter early by creating a new category or to enter once the new category has grown and is consolidated. To answer the question, we must first go back to review the difference between being a pioneer and an innovator. Pioneers are not reinventors. They create new stuff, but they don't successfully introduce it in the market. It could be because of its excessive price, because it is framed in a way that people don't find it valuable, or because the product might need some rework. On the other hand, there is the reinventor, who identifies a consumer problem and reinvents an existing product in a way that it becomes a mainstream product. The reinventor is the one who successfully introduces a product into the market.

Taking this into account, you shouldn't aspire to be a pioneer. You should aspire to be a reinventor. You should enter early into a market by launching a product that already has consumer traction.

Strategically, it is critical for a new venture to enter on the first stages of the development of the new category. Why? Because by entering early, a company can build a solid customer baseline over time, gain knowledge from customers to improve its products, and focus marketing efforts on being perceived as the leader and as the most relevant brand for a specific set of customers.

Now, imagine if a new venture enters the market once the category has developed. It would face at least one small brand with a loyal and significant customer baseline, and it would have to confront a big corporation with a gigantic advertising budget as well. Strategically, you don't want to put your company in that position.

Burton Snowboards is a company that was built by entering early in the market and leading a new category, snowboarding. In 1977, Jake Burton Carpenter launched one of the first modern snowboards, the Burton Backhill. But Burton did not invent the first snowboard deck. He was not the pioneer; he was the reinventor. The first snowboards were born in early 1910, when people used a flat wooden surface and a rope tied on the front of the deck to control its direction, a concept that evolved throughout years. By the mid-1960s, an engineer called Sherman Poppen designed the first modern snowboard, which he called the "snurfer," given that it allowed a surfer to glide over the snow. Poppen and his wife created the Brunswick Corporation to manufacture and sell snurfers across the country. It was a successful company that sold over one million snurfers over the following ten years.

However, the true reinventor was Jake Burton, who decided to change the product and transform it into a new sport. In the middle 1970s, snowboarding was just a hobby to people, a toy to have fun with. What Burton did differently was to focus on cultivating the sport itself. He wanted to become the leading brand within the snowboarding community. He even began manufacturing snowboards and quickly realized that people would also need footwear and outerwear to better perform the sport. Besides that, Burton began sponsoring the world's best snowboarders to build credibility and visibility of the brand.

By entering early into a market with proven consumer traction, Burton was able to become the leader in this new category and is still today enjoying a 33 percent share of the board market.

Another case of early entry in the market was the one made by the Leica brand. The Tourist Multiple is considered to be the first 35-mm camera. It was launched in 1913 by Herbert & Hugesson from New York. However, as I explained before, being first or the pioneer is not a guarantee of success. In fact, it carries several liabilities to overcome. For Herbert & Hugesson, this was no exception. The pricing was off the roof, selling each camera at $175, and the product needed considerable improvement. Film quality was poor. And to make matters worse, WWI was not helping the company take off in order to reach other exterior markets like Europe.[20]

It was not until Ernst Leitz, the founder of the Leica camera and the category creator, launched the first commercially successful 35mm camera in the spring of 1925 that portable cameras grew as a category.

Throughout those years in between, technology had advanced, and Leitz, from Leitz Optische Werke, identified its potential at the right time—that is, with the adequate technology to deliver a competitive price and a product that was known by consumers for its actual value, not its flaws.

The Leica camera was an immediate success. In 1926, more than one thousand cameras were manufactured, and in the following years, production doubled. By 1930, production reached an average of thirty thousand a year.

So you can confidently launch early as long as you can guarantee two things:

1. <u>Consumer traction can be identified:</u> Make sure there is an existing problem in the market that consumers are trying to solve inefficiently and that you are making use of a new technology to solve it in a unique way.
2. <u>There is no category leadership:</u> Your brand can still be associated as the category creator or leader. Your main goal will be to build and strengthen that link between your brand and the new category.

By launching early, a company will benefit from five key advantages.

<u>Positioning</u>
Reinventors have the advantage of being perceived as the category creators and leaders. This way, if a later entrant copies the same positioning strategy, it will probably be perceived as unauthentic and less credible.

<u>Technological Leadership</u>
The sooner you can start launching a product into the market, the quicker you will receive feedback to start capitalizing on this knowledge and improving your product.

<u>Brand Loyalty</u>
Fitbit, the early creator of the connected fitness and health category in 2007, goes beyond the functional benefit of tracking your daily physical activity. Fitbit built the largest community of users that encourage friendly competition to reach fitness goals. The brand also created Fitbit Challenges™ to keep users motivated, the same way they created achievement badges for people who reach certain milestones such as walking 100,000 daily steps. A brand that started selling their wristbands and watches was able to reinvent its functionality by connecting them to your mobile device, to social media, and to their community of users and is even partnering with other brands such as Microsoft's digital assistant, Cortana. It expands your fitness experience; it is not just a fitness tracking device. By entering early, they were able to grow an engaging community that generated

user loyalty and at the same time protects the brand from competitors.

Access

There is always limited space in distribution. No matter if you are a consumer goods company selling products on a super-market shelf, if you are a new restaurant chain, or if you are a gaming company, space is limited. Therefore, if you are able to enter early enough with something unique and new, it will be very difficult for a second entrant to get the same space in distribution.

Awareness

Press, social media, and word of mouth will quickly be interested in your story as long as you have reinvented something in a unique and valuable way for the consumer. Later entrants have a much more difficult task in cutting through the noise, especially because they have nothing new to explain. The innovator has created the category and is now considered the leader.

The Sholes and Glidden typewriter, also known as the Remington No. 1, was the first commercially successful typewriter. Launched on July 1, 1874, it is now celebrating its one hundred and fortieth anniversary. When the product was launched, consumers were not prepared for an immediate adoption. People needed training to know how to type, and it was not even considered respectful to send typed letters rather than handwritten ones. Besides, the first models needed some rework, and the price was $125, a cost that was as high as the average annual salary of a person at that time.

Only four hundred typewriters were sold by the end of the first year.[21] On the other hand, the nineteenth century brought about the ideal business environment for a typewriter. The pace of business was increasing, and also new technologies such as the telegraph and the telephone were being adopted by a growing number of companies. The typewriter was a solution that matched those needs.

So, by entering early, Remington benefited from two valuable outcomes:

1. They validated that there was consumer traction— that is, people trying to solve a problem inefficiently, which Remington identified and had the ideal technology to overcome.
2. It allowed the company to learn positive lessons from its first prototype. Once the product was improved and reduced its price in the following years, Remington was able to lead the category and protect itself against competitors.

In the following years, with the launch of the Remington 2, the company was able to triple the sales to 1,200 units. The typewriting industry had begun to develop, and Remington was ahead.

Enter early to own the category.

2.3. DESIGN
DESIGN IS NOT ONLY A SKIN

Design has always had a critical role in business. It was a design decision that Henry Ford made to create a single model in order to reduce manufacturing costs, and this allowed him to assemble an affordable car for the general public—a design that was subject to the egalitarian idea that everyone should have a car.

It was design again that reinvented the computer and the phone industries with the thoroughly designed iMac and iPhone.

First of all, we should all agree what design means. In many cases, companies think of design as a smart and good-looking skin built on top of a worn-out body and old engine. We usually think of design as the exterior image of a physical product and its packaging. The shell that covers the real product. An aesthetic feature rather than a functional one. Companies that think this way involve designers too late in the product development process. When they get to the final part, they expect designers to give it a cool look. Unfortunately, at that point, little can be done.

It turns out that design is larger than making things beautiful and cool. Design is a driving force that affects every business and every department, because design is about creating brand experiences between the company and the customer. Great design clarifies and delights consumer experiences.

Let's take, for instance, a product that everybody knows: the iPhone. Design is not only the way it looks but also the software that defines the way we text, the way we download apps, the way we browse the web, the way we listen to music, and the way we charge the phone every day. But I won't stop here. Design also affects how Apple stores are distributed, how people will pay, and what journey customers will follow. The same applies to the online Apple store: How difficult is it to find the product I am looking for? How many steps does a customer need to go through before pushing the buy button?

Bill Moggridge, cofounder of one of the most prominent design firms, IDEO, explains this holistic approach of design with one example. Moggridge was in charge of designing what is considered the first laptop computer in history. It was called the Grid Compass. From a product standpoint, he produced a design masterpiece. The computer was thin enough so that it could be transported inside a briefcase, it had a leg at the bottom so it could be used at the right angle, and it even had a magnesium body so when the machine wore out and the paint chipped off, the consumer could still see the nice magnesium body showing through.

However, when Moggridge received the first prototype, he soon realized that his work only represented the tip of the iceberg. As he describes it, "I found myself forgetting about my physical design, and realizing that everything I was interested in was happening behind the screen. I felt I was being sucked down inside the machine, and the interaction between me and the device was all to do with the digital software and very little to do with the physical design."[22]

Design needs to be connected with human behavior, no matter if it involves designing hardware or software. It all happens under the same discipline of interaction design.

For this reason, design should also influence other critical areas such as the purchasing, the support, and the exit experience. In other words, design should also influence customer service and the customer-brand relationships.

Some people call it "design thinking," and some other people call it "interaction design" because it defines the way a company thinks and interacts at every level. Therefore, design shouldn't be a silo. It should be a responsibility of each department.

Design is a strategic business area that has five clear purposes.

1. Communicate

We tend to think of communication as a series of advertising channels that companies have to get the word out, and frequently we forget that we own other cheap channels such as the product and packaging itself as a way of generating word of mouth and creating a brand image. Furthermore, the marketing investment required will be close to zero.

In the beverage industry, there is an example that illustrates the possibilities of design to create products that speak for themselves. On the packaging side, Innocent Drinks, which manufactures fruit smoothies, created labels that told stories. Think of a label as a movie or TV screen but is free. The space you have is essentially a free advertisement, an opportunity to talk about the drink. If the writing was interesting, people would read it the way they read other news on their mobile phones. By constantly changing the images and texts on the label, you would keep your product interesting. This is how

Innocent Drinks used design to start a conversation with customers and to show what is behind the brand.

Chipotle Mexican Grill restaurants even went a step further and recently invited famous authors to write essays on their bags and cups. The initiative was called "cultivating thought," and it originated after the *New York Times* best-selling author Jonathan Safran Foer had nothing to read while he was eating a burrito one day at Chipotle. He wrote to the CEO, Steve Ells, and suggested this idea of sharing short thoughts and stories by famous authors on its bags and cups.

You could read essays from Malcom Gladwell, author of *Tipping Point*, *Outliers*, and *Blink*, and Michael Lewis to Judd Apatow, writer/director/producer of *This Is 40*, *Bridesmaids*, and *Girls*.

On the product side, design allows us to reframe categories. Think of the Beats by Dr. Dre headphones. The company doesn't compete on sound; it doesn't even focus on a certain product feature in their advertising. Instead, Beats focuses on creating a brand that is associated with sports and fashion, a strategy that could only be achieved through an iconic headphone design.

Fit the design into the brand!

Design has a key role in branding, but the ultimate goal of design is to add value and fit the brand. Design is not an independent department that will work in an isolated way to come up with ideas that are aligned with the brand values.

The tequila company Patrón is a clear example of how design has to serve the brand. Patrón Tequila also created a new category, top-shelf tequila, a subcategory and premium space that it still leads since its creation, followed only by José Cuervo's range of less-expensive tequilas. Its high price, its quality, and even its bottle come together to build one of the most powerful brands today. It has even been named in rap songs and is being distributed in Canada with the help of one of the Blues Brother, Dan Aykroyd.

How did design help Patrón increase its brand status? As their billboards and magazine ads, claim, "No two bottles are exactly alike. So you can give all your friends something different. Eliminate regifting. Patrón Tequila is one-of-a-kind. Our signature blending of old and new world distillation techniques gives it an uncommon smoothness. Even our bottles are unique—each one handmade and individually numbered. The result is a gift people treasure rather than pass on." As the ads show, the handcrafted bottle design is probably one of the top assets of the brand now. But design even had a more critical role in the company's inception.

In 1989, John Paul DeJoria founded Patrón Spirits Co. with his friend Martin Crowley. Crowley was an architect who had gone to Mexico to buy stone pavers and furniture to sell to architects in the United States. DeJoria told Martin, "Why don't you bring back a few bottles of whatever the best tequila is that Mexicans drink down there?'"

Martin brought him back a Mexican tequila in a unique hand-blown bottle that impressed DeJoria. The bottle was outstanding, and the tequila tasted good. So DeJoria told Martin that if they could get it smoother and tastier, they could go into business and position the product as a premium liquor in the market.

The bottle design was and still is a key defining asset for the Patrón brand because it gave visual cues and supported the brand image: a handmade bottle for a handmade tequila, an attribute that is generally associated with top quality.

To achieve this brand personality through design, you must make sure your design is consistent over time. Only in this way will your brand be recognizable through design. Think of a Frank Gehry building, a Picasso painting, or a BMW car. They all have consistent and common attributes that you can quickly associate with the brand.

Yes, design has to serve the brand, but it has to remain consistent and repetitive over time if you want it to stick in people's minds. Only in this way will you develop a brand personality.

2. Create Loyalty

The way we interact with a product can also generate loyalty. Think of the Apple user interface. One of the reasons Apple fans stick to the brand is because they like and are highly familiar with their proprietary user interface. Apple uses the same menus for the iPhone, iPad, and iPod. How easy is it to buy a new gadget and from the moment you open it, you know you will be able to start using it?

On a deeper level, design can also build business platforms that create a stronger loyalty with a brand. iTunes was the music platform that Apple created to compete in the rapidly growing digital music market. The key ingredient was to design a user-friendly and intuitive music store together with a music device that could work in conjunction with the Apple software.

At that time, other brands such as the Sony MP3 were only offering a poor solution that allowed users to play dozens of songs. Not only that but the user interface made it difficult for users to download and administer songs. Furthermore, the music library was highly limited because Sony was afraid of cannibalizing its music label, Sony Music. In all, this generated a gap between what the market offered and what consumers demanded.

So, in an attempt to catch up, Apple acquired the SoundJam MP company, a small jukebox program for the Mac, and hired a top programmer named Jeff Robbin to simplify the music program into what it became and we all know as iTunes.

In the following years, all the Apple devices would connect to the same platform to manage songs and movies. But with what began as a music platform, Apple continued developing and promoting other platforms such as the App Store to integrate all the mobile devices.

Try to think about platforms more than about products. How can your company create a platform that consumers value and want to remain loyal to? Every product design presents an opportunity to create loyalty. And every company should aim at achieving a design or a shopping experience that makes people keep buying a certain brand.

Even the way we buy a sandwich can create loyalty. The Subway restaurant model creates loyalty. Fred DeLuca and Peter Buck, founders of Subway, designed their business model based on giving people the ability to customize their own sandwiches, to see the ingredients, and to watch the way they are assembled. Once customers are given that freedom and transparency, they become loyal to that way of creating sandwiches because it's unique.

3. Protect
Let's be honest: nowadays, more and more companies can copy an innovative concept in a quicker way. Once a company shows the first signs of success, dozens of imitators will quickly appear. And design has the ability to protect your brand and your product.

The key is to build a unique product that can be easily identified by consumers. The goal is to build a "smashable design," a design that can be identified by a consumer, even if someone threw the product against a wall and shattered it into small pieces.

The "smashable design" idea started to get traction with the growth of the first self-service grocery stores and supermarket chains in the early 1910s. Before supermarkets, people just went into a store and asked for a product, and the store manager would give them the only product he had. So people didn't really have to choose, and companies that manufactured products didn't feel the need to differentiate themselves.

However, things changed in the following years with the appearance of the first self-service grocery stores. In 1915, companies began to use design to differentiate their products and packaging. One of them was Coke.

At that time, soda bottles looked pretty much the same. You could only tell which brand it belonged to if you looked at the label. That was a temporary solution because it presented a problem: paper labels slid off when the bottle got wet when stocked between ice to kept it chilled. So consumers had to blindly fish around in the cold water and ice cubes to get the brand they wanted. There you have it—an inefficient way of doing things that presented an opportunity for innovative companies. So, at that point, Coke executives asked themselves, "What if our bottle was shaped in a different way?"

In 1915, The Coca-Cola Company organized a contest in which they asked to their bottlers to design a bottle shape that would be easily identified by consumers in the dark or even when the bottle was smashed to pieces.

Earl R. Dean, who worked at the Root Glass Company, wanted to emulate the shape of a kola nut. However, when he went to the library, he didn't find any images of it. The only picture he found was one of a cacao pod in the *Encyclopaedia Britannica*. So he used it to elaborate the design that became the contour bottle that has now been on the market for nearly one hundred years.

Today, brands face the same challenge. The Coke example might seem old and far away in time, but more recently Vitamin Water built an empire, in part thanks to creating an iconic bottle design that has kept imitators away. Now, Vitamin Water consumers can show with pride that they are drinking the real deal, the authentic and original drink, not a copy. This is the same way that Crocs built an entire business based on the unique design of comfortable shoes made out of rubber with holes.

Overall, brands need to create iconic and unique designs that are quickly identifiable by consumers. It is one of the most cost-effective and sustainable ways to protect a brand against imitators and competitors.

4. Solve Problems

Design can solve consumer problems, but it has its limits too. How to identify them? As I mentioned earlier, it is all about identifying consumer traction. Are consumers showing signs of solving a problem on their own? If there is no traction, it is difficult that a new design is accepted and used by the general public.

Imagine that every time you bought a computer, you had to learn the way that keys are placed on a keyboard. Instead of the standardized QWERTY keypad, a company created a more efficient layout. You would probably stick with the same brand to avoid that painful learning process.

We are creatures of habit, and once we grow used to a certain way of shopping, eating, or taking a picture, it is difficult to change behaviors. So when you design a new product or service, always try to keep it intuitive and natural. For instance, the gesture interface of an iPhone is new; it breaks the old pattern of moving through menus with the keyboard, but still gestures seem so intuitive and natural that they quickly become a new behavior.

So if you want to challenge the limits of design, make sure you do so because there is a significant consumer benefit or an imperative technical reason behind it; never change design for its own sake.

Digital cameras, for example, still have the same horizontal shape and proportion as the first analogue cameras that appeared. However, digital cameras don't have film to place inside, which is the main reason old cameras were shaped like a rectangle.

Now, as an entrepreneur, you should know that design does not have a mission on its own to just challenge the design for its own sake. Instead, a new design will be necessary when a new camera appears that can shoot and film in 360 degrees, such as the recently launched Bublcam camera or the Samsung Gear 360. In those cases, design had to challenge how traditional cameras are shaped. Behind any good design, there is a reason, a story.

5. Dynamize the Brand

The design process never ends. It is always a long journey. Even when you launch a new product, it will probably need to be improved with new technology advancements, and products will be updated with a new look. And this presents a new business opportunity.

This is what it is called dynamic obsolescence, the deliberate redesign of goods or services intended to render established goods and services outdated and eventually obsolete.

One of the earliest examples we find is in the automobile industry, a case that reframed the whole industry from a cost and uniform design manufactured by Ford to a colorful and fashionable design by General Motors (GM), transforming the automobile industry, especially for the benefit of GM, into a more dynamic and trend-driven consumer market.

Harley Earl, who inherited and worked at Earl Automobile Works, was the one responsible for implementing the dynamic obsolescence driven by design. In his early beginnings, his car workshop was already building customer bodies for Hollywood movie stars. He mastered design. However, his work influenced more than a series of producers and actors.

Earl Automotive Works was acquired by a Cadillac dealer who kept Earl as director of the custom body shop. But his innovative car design techniques gained more attention than he had ever imagined. Top Cadillac executives were amazed by his designs but also by the fact that he was using clay to develop the forms of his designs, something that no one had previously seen before. So, in 1927, he was assigned to build the LaSalle for Cadillac, a model that had such success that it attracted the attention of Alfred P. Sloan, the president of General Motors at that time. Sloan created a new department named the Art and Color Section of General Motors and made Earl its first director. From his new position, he was in charge of implementing Sloan's strategy of creating an annual model-year design to motivate car owners to replace their cars each year. And they integrated the body-on-frame chassis, which allowed the brand to more easily build new designs upon existing chassis rather than building a monocoque design used by most automakers. The small players in the industry could not follow their pace, and Ford didn't follow either because this dynamic vision went in the opposite direction of his. Henry Ford was focused on engineering, simplicity of design, and economies of scales to keep the costs down.

But in this case, design was the key ingredient that made General Motors the world leader in the automobile industry. Ford had been beaten up on their own terms: design.

For that reason, design should be considered as one of the most powerful ways to keep a brand dynamic. You need to aim at constant reinvention through design to keep your product relevant to your target market.

This is the next big topic I will cover: how can you make design work to deliver those multidimensional benefits for the brand? There are four considerations.

DESIGN FOR A GROUP, NOT FOR ALL

There is no objective reality. There are no best products or perfect products.

Imagine a chair. A chair cannot exist that feels comfortable to everyone in the world. People come in different sizes and shapes. No one knows this better than the industrial designer and pioneer in ergonomics, Henry Dreyfuss. In 1960, he published the book *The Measure of a Man*, now titled *The Measure of a Man and Woman*. In the book, Dreyfuss shows anthropometric charts of the range of dimensions of the human body parts so that industrial designers can use it to better adapt its product interaction and accommodation. With this book, a chair maker could comfortably design a chair made for a specific part of the population. However, to design a chair nearly close to perfection, it should be designed for only one person, completely customized. Consequently, the more you design a product or service that is based on the interests and priorities of a customer segment, the more your offering will satisfy them.

So, when creating a new product, your success will depend on being chosen by small number of consumers, therefore creating an offering and a design that is highly relevant to them and that adapts to their lifestyle, paying attention to the interaction with their peers rather than aiming to own the whole market and designing a product that tries to satisfy the whole population.

Taking a whole population into account or an average customer profile as a reference is useless. However, it is a common practice in the business world to create an image of the average customer, a description that goes something like this: "Joe is thirty-four years old. He has 1.8 kids, he drives to work, and he practices sports 2.5 days a week."

Why should someone care about an average Joe, who clearly does not exist? Instead, you have to look at extremes. If you lead a sports drink company, you should not be interested in making a difference in an average life. You should be focused on making a significant difference in a small group that really cares about running.

You have to look at the person who runs seven days a week, the sports animal. As Dan Formosa from Design & Research Smart Design New York says, "If we understand what the extremes are, the middle will take care of itself."

The Dangers of *Not* Designing for the Extremes

Design adds value when it is made around certain needs of a community of users, so to one extreme of the population. But what are the risks of not doing it?

This can be explained through one of the biggest product failures in modern history, the Sony eVilla. It only lasted two and a half months in the market.

The breakthrough idea of the eVilla was to transform the computer into a device that acted as a web and e-mail station. The traditional rectangular screen was replaced by a vertical one to better display and be able to read websites, a fifteen-inch Trinitron screen turned on its side. The theory was that the "Sony's eVilla unit eliminated the common hassles of connecting to the Internet, like having to boot up and dial in just to see if there's new e-mail, or trying to manage multimedia plug-ins," according to Mark Viken, president of Sony Electronics' Personal Network Solutions Company.

The eVilla could handle simple browsing, but the unit was not prepared to smoothly run videos and animation at Flash-intensive sites. In fact, animation did not match the audio smoothly. But more unforgivable was the fact that it did not support Shockwave or Microsoft Windows Media either. The dial-up connection was not quick enough to download MP3 files, and the audio from the built-in speakers was poor.

In all, it was a sound solution for people who only wanted basic access to the Internet and e-mail because it failed in all other fronts of computer function that a low-cost PC could do better. The product was launched on June 14, 2001, and it was removed from the market on August 30, 2001.

The Sony eVilla should have been built to be the king of the Internet. It even had the screen turned upside down to succeed. However, it only offered value to light Internet users, not the heavy Internet users who would have embraced this new product, promoted it with their positive reviews, and paid the extra price for the unique product features and performance. Sony forgot to design for the most extreme users, which immediately would have made light users also part of its customer base.

DESIGN SHOULD SIMPLIFY

Simplicity is the hardest math in product design because it involves subtracting, prioritizing, and trading off product features.

Simplicity should be treated as a requirement to succeed because it has an increasing importance in people's lives today. We live in the culture of speed: customers read the first words of a customer review, they watch the first seconds of a YouTube video, and venture capitalists give you one minute to explain your strategy, vision, and growth plan. Speed is the norm. And simplifying allows you to focus like a laser beam on the added value of your product, at the same time making it clear for the consumer to understand.

People will understand the new concept faster and will find it a solution ten times better than any other product on the market. Simplicity not only sells, but it also sticks in the mind of the consumer.

If Ferrari were to come out with an advertising campaign introducing a new family safety system, it would definitely not help position the brand as a high-performance, head-turning sports car. Design is about making tradeoffs, something that will help you get closer to being remarkable at the one thing you are focused on.

So focus on stuff that people will use and that makes your product unique. The HD Hero GoPro camera only requires one button to record and stop. To play the Flappy Bird mobile game, you only need one finger. Google's landing page is as simple as an empty box that allows you to search for anything, and Instagram stylizes your pictures with only one click. They all have been geniuses in creating products that are so simple that they become unique solutions in the mind of a consumer.

So why have so many products become so complex? Let's travel back in time and see how the first microwave looked. It was a square box with three buttons to adjust the power (low, medium, high) and a timer. Now, things are quite different. We live in a culture where companies think that more is better. Even as consumers, we tend to compare products that way, the "how-much-it-costs-and-what-features-it-has" mentality.

Companies think that by adding more product features, it will provide them a greater advantage over their competitors. That happens with microwaves and with operating systems like Windows. Consequently, you end up with a more expensive product with piled-on, complex functionalities and features that nobody wants.

Therefore, the opportunities for applying simplicity to design are endless. Nokia, a brand that has lost relevancy in modern countries, has been winning in developing countries such as India and Brazil thanks to using simplicity. Nokia's ethnographers studied how technology could make the lives of workers in India and Brazil easier. Researchers found out that the regular phones were too expensive to buy and too flashy for a use that involved dust and no electricity to charge them. So, taking these insights into account, Nokia came up with a new phone, the Nokia 1100, a rugged mobile with a very simple design that allowed people to call and text in any climate condition and that could be charged up in a few minutes. It also has an additional lamp that helps workers see in low-light environments. The product was an instant hit. Since its launch in 2003, it has sold over 250 million units around the world, making it the best-selling mobile ever.[23]

But design should not stop at creating a simplified product; it should also help in defining and simplifying the whole buying process. Design should also be aimed at improving decision speed—in other words, in reducing the time it takes consumers to go from being aware of the product to actually buying it.

As Frank W. Woolworth, founder of the Woolworth discount stores, said, "I am the world's worst salesman; therefore, I must make it easy for people to buy." You have to design shopping experiences and products that are easy to buy and are enjoyable. Don't sell the customer. Help him buy.

Think of the last time you visited Amazon.com to buy something you liked. How easy was it to find it? And how easy was it to complete the buying process? I hope you agree it was a fairly easy task because that is what Amazon does best. It eliminates friction between what you want to buy and the "place the order" button. It eliminates steps. Amazon is focused on the buy. No matter if you are an online or a traditional merchant, you have to focus on reducing friction, on simplifying the buying process. Think about Amazon again. Can prospects sample the product or service? Yes, they can. You can look into books and watch additional product pictures and videos. Can prospects read an objective product review to reduce uncertainty? Yes, they can.

The role of design in simplifying products and the shopping experience is critical. It is not only about looking nice, polished, and uncluttered but also about selling more.

FRUGALITY IN DESIGN
Nowadays, it is a common practice to grow a business with the backing of a private investor, VC firm, or bank to develop the idea, put the product on the market, and finally to promote it to stand out in the market and create customers. However, in emerging markets, there is a growing trend that goes in the opposite direction, a growing way of doing things where anything can be built using the available technology or resources in a new and smart way. It was called "jugaad innovation" by Navi Radjou, Dr. Jaideep Prabhu, and Dr. Simone Ahuja.[24]

Jugaad innovation is frugal innovation at its purest state, and it is having a huge impact on hundreds of millions of people. Even global corporations have already tried to copy this technique. "Jugaad" is a Hindi word that translates as "an innovative fix; an improvised solution born from ingenuity and cleverness."[25] It is about doing more with less, and it is practiced every day in countries like India, China, Africa, and Brazil. In China, they call it *zizhu chuangxin* and in Kenya *jua kali*.

Why is this important for any reinventor? Because it challenges what can be done with no resources at all. It challenges the preconceived mental frameworks in which we are used to solving problems. And it is definitely a reference to take into account when solving consumers' problems in a way that is accessible to them.

Let There Be Light

How can an empty bottle of Coke become the main source of light in an underprivileged house in the Philippines? In the Philippines' slums, many people cannot afford the cost of having artificial light at home. Furthermore, during the day, those families don't have enough light inside their houses. The roofs are made of corrugated metal, and windows are tiny or nonexistent to protect them from the wind, rain, and cold weather. So the jugaad innovator Illac Diaz came up with the idea of using an empty Coke bottle, filling it with bleach-treated water, and installing it in a hole in the roof of each house. The water in the bottle refracts the sun's rays, producing the equivalent of a fifty-five-watt light bulb. This light cost just one dollar, and it also generates jobs in the community because it needs someone to install it. The solar bottle bulb (SLB) has already been installed in more than one million homes across the Philippines.[26]

Clearly, not all businesses can create such a frugal product, but at least every new business should try to challenge the current industry frameworks, the current way of solving problems.

No Craftsmanship, No Problem—for Five Dollars It Can Be Learned

In 1977, Ben and Jerry were two high-school friends living together in upstate New York. They knew they wanted to build a store together, but they had no clue in which market. They had no jobs and nothing to lose. They loved food, so making some sort of food product would make sense to them. However, they did not have any extraordinary craftsmanship skills. So they looked into two products they thought could be relatively easy to learn about and execute: bagels and ice cream. The bagel business involved way more costs in equipment than ice-cream manufacturing, so the answer was clear. They took a five-dollar correspondence course from Penn State University, and since they were broke at that time, they split one course between them. Later that year, Ben and Jerry persuaded their relatives to give them a loan, which, combined with their micro savings, allowed them to start up their own ice-cream shop. They found a store in Vermont where they didn't find any competitors. Their philosophy was that because they had no idea what they were doing, they would be much more successful without any other ice-cream shop around, even though Vermont is a very cold place with a long winter—not the obvious place to locate an ice-cream business.

They built the store from scratch with their hands. It took them five months. And all the ice cream was manufactured by hand too. On May 5, 1978, they opened their first store. The ice cream was a hit. Within a few hours, long lines of customers trailed out of the door.

So even if you don't consider yourself a talented craftsman, you can still build your business with your own hands. It will definitely help anyone understand the business from the bottom up, be inventive, create a unique product, and save thousands of dollars that you can better invest in inventory, machinery, or even events to bring people together and get the word out.

THE IRONY OF THINKING DIFFERENTLY IN DESIGN

Imagine there is a company that launches a new product. However, this product uses several features and functionalities from competing brands. To promote it, the company creates a marketing campaign that includes a TV commercial practically identical to that of another brand. Now, what if I told you this company's main claim is about thinking differently? Yes, I am talking about Apple and one of its most successful products, the iPod.

Steve Jobs himself, in a 1996 interview, said, "Picasso had a saying: 'Good artists copy; great artists steal.'" Apple has always been shameless about stealing great ideas. For the iPod, Apple borrowed groundbreaking features like the "click and tactile wheel" from industry pioneers such as Diamond Multimedia and Creative Labs.

With regard to iPod´s first TV, print, and outdoor ad campaign, you just have to watch the Lugz boots brand TV ad aired from August until December 2002 to realize the resemblance with Apple's black dancing silhouettes "original" idea— one of Apple's most iconic advertising campaigns. You draw your own conclusions. Both commercials show black silhouettes of people dancing in an urban setting with rap music on the background using the same colors (red, orange, yellow, and black). However, a Chiat/Day art director is believed to have come up with the design of the iPod silhouette commercials, which were broadcast in the fall of 2003.

When we call something "original," it is just because we are not aware of the references and the sources, even when companies claim to "think different."

As William Ralph Inge said, "What is originality? Undetected plagiarism."

Remember: reinvent; don't invent.

Part 3

ENGAGE

I have always considered that the word "advertising" is a term that refers to a monologue initiated by a company trying to sell stuff to a group of people. Instead, I think advertising should be considered a dialogue with people. It should represent a way of engaging with them.

In the next chapters, I will cover why advertising needs to evolve and what opportunities engagement will deliver to brands that want to create a new space in the market.

3.1. THE FALL OF ADVERTISING TO BUILD A BRAND

We live in a cycle of distrust. People have become distrustful and cautious. Everyone is looking for the trap, not only at an advertising level but also on a quality level after some food scandals and security breaches in major social media sites.

Dan Ariely, a psychology and behavioral professor at Duke University and author of the book *Predictably Irrational*, organized a research study that proved this point. The experiment consisted of measuring to which extent people trusted offers and advertising. The researches set up a booth at a big shopping mall with a sign that read "Free Money" and a smaller sign that indicated the amount of money they were giving away. The amount of money varied over time from one dollar to five dollars and sometimes ten, twenty, or up to fifty dollars.

When people passed by, they were suspicious about the offer, but still some of them took it. To be specific, only 1 percent grabbed the one-dollar bill, and the percentage went up until it got to fifty dollars, when only 19 percent took it. So taking into account that it was literally free, I think you would agree that this is not a high level of success. So researchers asked people who had looked at the booth and continued walking why they hadn't stopped. All the answers were the same; respondents were dubious about the offer, and they believed that there was some sort of scheme.

You cannot launch a small brand with advertising because it has no credibility, it is not a scalable strategy, and traditional ads will never return more than you have invested in them. Instead, a new venture should focus on building a marketing machine that provides a positive feedback loop. In other words, an entrepreneur should focus on creating product news, events, and content that people are willing to share and cover on social media. A small brand should focus on creating amazing product features, delivering extraordinary customer service, providing spreadable digital content (videos, social media posts), and writing articles that can become viral hits in order to get more eyeballs than investing in traditional channels.

Advertising is only worth it for one purpose, to maintain its visibility once a brand has been created by other techniques such as public relations, word of mouth, grassroots events, and social media. For instance, Starbucks, Amazon.com, Google, Red Bull, GoPro, and The Body Shop have been built with practically no advertising at all. In the case of The Body Shop, its founder, Anita Roddick, got global media coverage when she traveled around the world looking for the best ingredients for her natural cosmetics products.

Advertising is overrated. Start engaging with people.

3.2. BRAND CONTACT POINTS

*Managing brands is going to be more
and more about trying to manage
everything that your company does.*

—*LEE CLOW, CHAIRMAN OF TBWA\
MEDIA ARTS LAB*

I don't like to call it advertising. I like to call it engaging with consumers.

Advertising is an old silo with a very limited area of influence. It does not take into consideration other areas where consumers connect with the brand, which are:

- Customer care
- Public relations
- Branded content
- Grassroots marketing
- Endorsements
- Virality

CUSTOMER CARE

The interaction between the brand and a prospective buyer or a current customer is usually underestimated and is consequently not seen as a way of driving sales and creating long-term customers.

Customer care is seen as a cost on a company's balance sheet. Therefore, as all costs do, they have to be reduced year over year. The result is obvious: complex processes to get in touch with the company and ineffective customer solutions. If you want to get in touch with a customer representative, you will probably have to spend quite a long time looking for a solution in the frequently asked questions (FAQ) section or filling in a complex complaint survey that might take one week to get an answer from.

However, there are companies that see it differently. In 2009, Best Buy launched Best Buy Twelpforce, a Twitter account that helps solve customers' problems instantly and on a social network they already know. eBay, the online auction site, took it a step further, creating on-location conferences to give new sellers and top sellers proven strategies to be more successful on eBay. Furthermore, they uploaded all the conferences on YouTube so any eBay member could benefit from them.

Think of customer care as an engagement channel, as a way of establishing a proactive, long-term relationship with a customer and as a way of generating priceless word-of-mouth recommendations.

> *It is so much easier to be nice, to be respectful,*
> *to put yourself in your customers' shoes and*
> *try to understand how you might help them*
> *before they ask for help than it is to try to*
> *mend a broken customer relationship.*

> —MARK CUBAN, BUSINESSMAN, INVESTOR, AND
> OWNER OF THE NBA's DALLAS MAVERICKS.

PUBLIC RELATIONS: BUILDING THE BUZZ

I believe that getting your business covered by nationwide media is one of the most misleading communication activities. Let's be honest: nearly any type of new venture can appear in the technology or business section of an influential newspaper or blog. Is it worth it? Definitely it is. Media presence drives up awareness. A business can gain visibility among investors and the community in general, but it doesn't have value beyond that. Furthermore, it only represents a temporary spark, and taking into account the number of news stories that appear every day, it will just vanish the following day. So don't confuse appearing in the media at a certain moment in time with driving up sales because you will regret the amount of hours you have dedicated to getting your business covered.

The key is to focus all the energy on figuring out the story that you want to share. Because once you elaborate the winning story, people will want to know more about it and will probably engage with your business as a spokesperson and as a customer.

How to elaborate a long-lasting story? First, this should be an entrepreneur's job. You want it to be authentic, and even if writing is not your strength, you should become the storyteller-in-chief. So what are the common characteristics of a memorable story?

A. Think of the General Public:
You represent a new brand with an innovation that might only interest a fraction of the population, but when it comes to

storytelling, you have to appeal to the whole population. You will achieve that by using emotions. Emotions are universal; they generate interest at a human level no matter which country you are from. What grabs people's attention are emotional, self-expressive, and social benefits.

Spanx is a universal story that illustrates this point. Sara Blakely, founder of the innovative body-shaping undergarment brand Spanx, framed her story using the classic example of David versus Goliath. She framed herself as a regular woman who, one day before going to a party, realized that she couldn't put on some new cream pants because she didn't know what to put underneath. Traditional shapers were too thick, and underwear left a panty line. So Blakely decided to cut the feet out of pantyhose and put them on under her new pants. She felt great and was without any visible panty lines, so she thought, "This should exist for women." Straightaway, without business studies or professional fashion design experience, she decided to design the seamless pantyhose and patent it. She visited numerous fabric mills to help her put her design into production, but no company believed a seamless a panty could be done. It was an experience that opened her eyes to see that it was a multi-million-dollar male-dominated industry that didn't value someone with no experience and no money to invest—until suddenly she found a mill owner who trusted her because his daughter had told him that the product made a lot of sense and was unique.

This story illustrates the emotion behind the product idea, which came after realizing a problem she encountered herself. There is a self-expressive benefit when she shows her perseverance and her ability to face down doubters and those who laughed at her. And there is a social benefit when the product was actually made, and millions of women around the world could benefit from it, from Oprah Winfrey to Gwyneth Paltrow.

B. Frame the Story around a New Category, Not a Product

Every entrepreneur is tempted to start talking about how great his or her product is. However, journalists are tired of hearing from self-promoting people. They are looking for bigger stories that will actually interest their readers.

Therefore, you should frame your story as the creator of a new category that will change how people are doing some sort of thing. You want to create debate. Do you people want to read about the technical specifications of a new product called an e-book? Or do they want to read about how books could disappear with the arrival of the e-books?

As a category leader, you may find that it is far more appealing to focus on the category and its impact on people's daily routines and lifestyles because the brand that leads this category will capitalize on all the attention. And because a new category can have different story angles, you should also consider elaborating on a story that exploits the intersection between several trends that are grabbing media attention. The mobile app to book hotels, HotelTonight.com, could generate interest if it was framed around mobile applications, the emergence of "deal" websites, the "instant commerce" trend, or impromptu traveling. Each angle will be more interesting for different kinds of media because it will be more relevant to their readers.

C. Generate Momentum

Something has to happen at a certain point in time. You cannot just share a story without a significant date. Otherwise, journalists will feel they can publish the story anytime they want. So, by creating an event such as a product launch, you will force journalists and bloggers to cover your business at the same time, consequently generating positive momentum. You will coordinate the buzz. And buzz leads to more buzz because people and journalists don't want to be left out of what's happening right now.

Contrarily, leaving freedom as to when to publish your story will thinly spread its impact over time, and the result will be individual small bursts rather than a big ball of fire. One hundred people talking about something over the course of one month pales in comparison to one hundred people talking about it in one day.

D. Be Your Own Publicist

Media doesn't write about you. One writer does. Now, imagine that you are a journalist. Would you rather get a call or e-mail from a PR agency or from someone who is the founder of a new company that is disrupting an industry? Besides, stories can also be told on television, not only in printed media. And no one else can do that job for you.

Everything a brand does is telling a story.

BRANDED CONTENT

Creating and distributing branded content is also a powerful marketing strategy. A brand could create a video to use it as a manifesto to communicate its values, add value to the end user by showing its product features, or communicate new product releases.

People might think that content marketing is the latest digital gimmick. But in fact, in 2015, digital media grew 17.2 percent to nearly $160 billion and is forecasted to keep growing by 13.5 percent in 2016. It is expected to overtake TV (a $503 billion global ad market) as the biggest advertising category by the end of 2017, the forecast says.[27] And this trend is showing no signs of slowing down anytime soon, given its double-digit growth over the last years. Furthermore, content marketing has been taking place since a long time ago—and not necessarily within digital channels. One of the first entrepreneurs to use this tool was Walt Disney.

Walt had always been a pioneer and an innovator by embracing new technology that could make his company's animations more vibrant and unique. When TV came out, he was also able to come up with a winning formula to promote his films.

In 1954, he began hosting a TV series called "Disneyland," where Walt presented how his studio produced animated cartoons, and he also included some teasers of recent and upcoming films such as *Alice in Wonderland*. It represented the first TV show produced by a movie studio. After its success, the rest of the industry—MGM, 20th Century Fox, and Warner Bros.—also decided to produce their own TV shows. These copies didn't last very long. None of them had the charisma and energy of Walt.

Now, in the digital age, content marketing has exploded given that anyone can upload a video online, write a post on any social media platform, and publish an article on their blogs. There are no limits. The filter is not distribution; the filter is creating new, unique, and engaging content that people like and are willing to share.

The challenge today is being listened to, because any brand can have a voice. However, some brands are lazy; they have forgotten the real key to creating viral branded content. Most of the brands now think, *Why spend time and money on a fun or meaningful campaign when you can just get your intern to throw up posts like "Share this on your wall and enter to win a one-dollar gift card"?* If your brand is headed this way, forget saying you are creating content. You will just be rumbling in a loud marketplace.

Red Bull has mastered the art of creating content that people want to engage with and share—from filming and sharing the action-sports events they organize to creating breathtaking videos that become viral hits. Their commitment is so strong that in 2007, they launched a production company named Red Bull Media House that is in charge of all this content creation.

Content might be a capital-intensive investment, especially at the beginning when the audience is still small, but it is definitely a highly influential, credible, and personality-defining marketing tool for the medium and long terms.

Given that it is a significant investment, many people wonder if a company should charge for its content. For example, should TED, the nonprofit conference organization, give away its conferences on YouTube, taking into account that people pay thousands of dollars to attend? Companies should stay focused on selling their products and services. Content is a pull strategy to drive people into the brand, to generate interest and visibility. The end goal should remain the same; for this reason content should be free. It should be an open gate for people to learn more about the brand.

Now, if you give away content, it is because you have a purpose in mind. And that is what should be defined from the start. In the case of TED, the goal should be to increase the number of people who attend their conferences. When people watch a talk, they want more; they want to get involved and support those ideas by sharing them. Then those people will tell others, and that is how it will spread. The result is an upward spiral. Instead of destroying demand to attend the live conferences, it increases the demand for it. Today, there are more than 1,500 talks available online, and they have been viewed over 600 million times by people around the world. Now, thanks to the globalization of the brand, TED was able to exponentially grow its number of conferences with the sub-brand TEDx, which allows any city or local community to organize its own event.

Definitely, for TED, it made sense to film a conference that was going to take place anyway and upload it online since the cost of doing so was marginal. What TED risked was that people decided not to go to its live events anymore. However, the opposite happened; it built global demand.

For Red Bull, the goal should be to keep the brand closely associated with extreme sports in order to be perceived as the leader of the energy drink category as well as to sell more Red Bull cans throughout the world. To the present day, the brand holds the largest market share worldwide.

Create an immersive brand experience through content.

GRASSROOTS MARKETING

Smalls brands are built from the bottom up. It is about interacting with and adding value to a small community through an initiative or service.

Grassroots is a highly convenient strategy for small brands because it is low-cost and because of its high impact on and relevance to the end consumer. You don't compete with dollars. You want people to feel something emotional about your brand.

Marc Ecko, founder of the urban clothing brand Marc Ecko, has always been a great supporter of grassroots campaigns, and in fact he produced several of the largest publicity stunts of the decade. In 1997, he couldn't afford to go to a menswear industry show in Las Vegas called Magic Show; they could only pay for the space to install a booth, but he had no money to build it. So he decided to go anyway and think of another promotional tactic. They printed twenty-five thousand bumper stickers that read "Where's Ecko?" and sent out a street team to distribute them around the exhibition. He ended up making more noise and sales doing this commando-style action than he had in the previous year with no presence at all.

In 2006, Ecko broke the rules again. He rented a Boeing 747 and hired a team to repaint it to look like Air Force One.

Then he pretended that a group of hooded people broke into a military base and sprayed the words "Still Free" on one side of Air Force One while a cameraman filmed all the action and posted it on YouTube. It represented one of the first viral videos on YouTube that spread like gunpowder because people thought it had been a real security breach at Andrews Air Force Base.

The resulting publicity was astonishing. Media jumped into the story to question if it was real or fake. It brought a huge jump in visibility to the brand. Furthermore, the action showed the values of the brand: transgressive, outspoken, and urban. As Ecko states, "I can't outdo Nike; I can't outfashion Ralph; I can't outsex Calvin. I'd much rather have a brand point of view that may make you scratch your head but is brand defining."

Start-ups from the digital world can also use this strategy to generate visibility and energize a brand. Uber, the disruptive private cab service based on an app, timed the release of the TV series "Boardwalk Empire" to offer New Yorkers vintage "gangster-style" rides. On Presidents' Day in Washington, DC, Uber offered a motorcade with American flags. One out of twenty orders that day got the Ubercade. Consequently, people who got those unique experiences shared them on social media platforms, getting high positive mentions. The word spread across the whole country.

It is not what a company does with a brand; it is what people do with the brand. Let them play with it, engage with it, so they can feel it's theirs and share it.

Some companies like Red Bull go even further. Not only do they create these fun and emblematic events like the Flugtag

(Flying Day), when people compete to fly the farthest over water in homemade flying machines, but they also hire undergraduate students as ambassadors of their brand to manage the Red Bull brand in universities. This role is what Red Bull calls brand managers, and they look for candidates at three hundred universities and colleges. They look for leaders who have enthusiasm for the brand and plenty of energy to do tasks such as identifying key groups on the campus, building image via Red Bull-owned events, building relationships that secure Red Bull properties via the campus media, assisting local sales team to ensure perfect distribution and visibility around the campus, and even submitting activities through pictures and reports—the best commando action a brand could get.

In all, grassroots marketing is about identifying local people with a shared interest for whom the brand can create a common, passionate, and ownable cause.

Ignore the conventional wisdom, and play the game by very different rules.

ENDORSEMENTS
<u>Why Small Brands Love the Pitchman</u>
When a brand partners up with a personality, it is mainly because it pursues one main goal: the brand wants to be associated with an aspirational role model relevant to the target market. By doing that, the brand wants to be energized by these personality traits.

An example that clearly illustrates this point is the successful video game Dr. J and Larry Bird, released by Electronic

Arts (EA) in 1983. It was as aspirational as it could get. At that time, computer graphics only allowed putting some pixels together, making the game characters indistinguishable. Then players at home had to imagine that one of the NBA characters was Dr. J and the other one was Larry Bird. Gamers could only tell because they saw their names and some photos of them playing basketball on the cover of the video game, but they loved it. After its success, Trip Hawkins, founder of EA, had the vision to continue creating more video games using the star power of personalities. As a result, he packaged the games with covers that looked like record albums.

This is an extreme case. But what it demonstrates is the influential power of those two big basketball stars to sell the game. If the game had been named Basketball, I bet it would have only sold a fraction of what it had. Kids would have lacked the aspiration to imagine they were Larry Bird or Dr. J while playing.

This is what Phil Knight, founder of Nike, calls the "pyramid of influence." Knight believed that people could be influenced by what top athletes were wearing and would buy sports shoes accordingly.

In February 2005, Nike launched a national TV campaign to promote the Air Jordan XX to celebrate the twentieth anniversary of Nike's most significant partnership in history. Nike is Jordan, and Jordan is Nike. Nike turned Jordan into the biggest athlete brand on earth, and Jordan turned Nike into a cultural icon. Jordan has been an absolute win, but what is most important is the endorsement and grassroots strategy behind this relationship.

It was Sonny Vaccaro, a self-made man who was a pro gambler in Las Vegas in 1977, who saw the opportunity to build some prototypes of a sandal-like basketball shoe and pitch it to different sports companies to get them investing and developing his idea. One of the companies he met with was Nike. Even though the Oregon-based shoe company was not interested in his product, it became interested in knowing more about his vision of basketball, a sport that apparently Vaccaro had a lot of knowledge about. At that time, Nike was strong on creating and marketing running shoes, and it was considering breaking into the basketball market. Vaccaro suggested that Nike pay college basketball coaches to put Nike shoes on their players. At that time, this was an innovative idea; no other companies were focusing their efforts in this direction, and therefore the company wouldn't have to pay the coaches much. College basketball teams benefited from being supplied professional shoes, and Nike benefited from using them as sports pitchmen. In this way, Nike created its pyramid of influence.

By the mid-1980s, after implementing Vaccaro's strategy, Nike boosted its basketball shoe sales from $7 million to $400 million per year. That growth spiral was what allowed Nike to sign the twenty-one-year-old Michael Jordan in 1984. Yet Nike broke the rules again because at that time no one was putting so many eggs in the same basket. Nike made a huge commitment investing $500,000 to sign Jordan—an unheard-of price for an endorsement.

But as Nike had done before, they offered Jordan his own signature shoe, in this way making Jordan a long partner with the Nike brand. It was a promise that its main competitor,

Adidas, wouldn't match. "Michael Jordan's last game was in 2003 and yet the Jordan brand sales keep growing. Brand Jordan today sells twice as much product around the world as when he was playing."[28]

It seems as if personality endorsements are something only big corporations can participate in, but this is not necessarily true. In the early 1970s, before it was a big brand, Nike began sponsoring runners like Steve Prefontaine, an athlete that Bill Bowerman, cofounder of Nike and a running coach, knew very well. He thought it would help give credibility to the brand.

Throughout history, we have seen many examples of small brands creating extraordinary win-win relationships with personalities, such as Powell Peralta with the Bones Brigade, Churchkey beer with the actor Adrian Grenier, Jimmy Choo and Tamara Mellon, or Honest Diapers with Jessica Alba. Strange as it might seem, all these companies were not as big as they are today at the time they signed with all these influential names. So how did they do it? What is the common ruling principle that made all these brand endorsements succeed? The key was to establish a win-win situation.

As a small brand, you have to establish a relationship that adds true value to the pitchman. In some cases, they might want to invest in the company like Jessica Alba did with Honest Diapers, a collection of completely toxin-free household cleaning products, diapers, and wipes. In other cases, the entrepreneur can add value by sponsoring an athlete and helping him or her grow to a professional level, the same way a small brand wants to have a bigger impact on consumers' lives.

Now, here is a big red flag: the brand must always take the lead and have the final cut on any decision. Therefore, I do not suggest in any case giving excessive power to a pitchman. Before partnering up, responsibilities have to be set point by point in a clear manner so that everyone builds realistic expectations around an agreement.

People tend to get overambitious over time. When they see money coming in, they will start trying to renegotiate, trying to invalidate the contract by claiming it is not fair or is legally invalid, or employing many other gimmicks to get as much as they can from you. This should not be the norm, but sadly it is. There is always a downside, and in this case it is better to be prepared for the worst than to remain naïve and be attacked by surprise.

The "You" Celebrity

The risks of partnering with an external pitchman lead us to an alternative strategy for entrepreneurs who might not find value in the pitchman for their particular business or because they feel that the risk of giving control to a spokesperson is way too high.

The alternative is that the entrepreneur becomes the brand's spokesperson. It won't cost you money, you control the message, it's authentic, and it is a long-term strategy because you will be able to capitalize on all the previous media coverage.

However, it demands that you walk into the spotlight, even if it's not in your nature. The key is to be who you are and don't play anyone else's game. If you are worried that you might not have enough charisma, think of John Schnatter, founder of Papa John's Pizza. The best Papa John's commercials feature Schnatter. He is a likable person who comes across as an ultra-ordinary guy. He even openly claims in several media interviews that he scored 200 out of 800 on his SAT verbal test.

Think of the pitchman as the narrator of your brand story. Whether it is an external spokesperson or you, the pitchman should be authentic.

VIRALITY
Viral Inflection Point

There is a moment in time when an under-the-radar brand will be moving forward to become a visible brand. Chances are high that when this occurs, it will be because you have reached a viral inflection point.

By viral, I am not referring to creating viral YouTube videos. I am talking about creating a viral strategy—a strategy that can lead into product platforms and campaigns that resonate with people and spread like the following case illustrates.

Alain Afflelou, the French optical chain, changed its growth pace thanks to a new promotion platform called "La moitié de votre monture à l'oeil" (that would translate into English as "Half of your frames for free"). It was not until this moment in time in 1978, six years after opening the first store, that the business really took off. The campaign was financed by all three stores, still a considerably small brand by then. The campaign allowed the business to sell around one hundred glasses a day. Also, thanks to its success, the positive results allowed Afflelou to start building Alain Afflelou as a franchise business, unifying store designs and product portfolios under one brand. A promotion was built upon the vision that prescription glasses should be more like fashion accessories rather than simple necessities. One consumer could have different glasses for home, work, or a party, a vision that inspired similar viral promotional platforms like the iconic platform called "tchin-tchin," launched in 1999, where consumers could buy a second pair of glasses for only one more franc. Today, Alain Afflelou has 1,100 stores around Europe, generating more than 850 million euros in sales.

Small brands need viral strategies to speed up growth. However, viral strategies cannot be managed independently. Small brands should first build a new solution to a consumer's problem, which creates a new category. Only then will a company be able to effectively implement a viral strategy to boost its visibility and speed of growth. There has to be a strong product that people demand and want to repurchase; otherwise, a business won't be able to monetize this peak of attention.

Viral Strategies in the Digital World
In the digital world, viral strategies have to be looked at from a different angle than traditional media because, in this case, speed of growth has a major role in a brand's success.

A viral strategy mainly serves two purposes: reducing the copycat risk and getting more bang for the buck from the communications budget. First, there is a high risk of other

start-ups cloning a business in a matter of weeks in the country where you operate, which would grab a considerable share
of potential users. Second, cash is usually short during the
launching phase. So brands must look at alternative ways of
capturing more attention than what you could have gotten
through traditional advertising and media channels, where
you only get the amount of impact that you pay for.

The father of the modern viral campaign is Hotmail.
com, and again they didn't use any viral video at all. In 1996,
Sabeer Bhatia and Jack Smith launched a new web-based
e-mail site that offered users new accounts. During the first
months, the growth was sluggish, and with only a limited
investment from the venture capital firm Draper Fisher
Jurvetson, the team could not afford a traditional advertising campaign, where you get the number of eyeballs based
on the amount of money you invest. What the team did was
to add a message at the bottom of every single e-mail, "P.S.
Get your free e-mail at Hotmail," with a link to the website.
Within days, the product tweak produced massive results.
Within six months, more than one million users had signed
up. Eighteen months after launching the start-up and having
reached twelve million subscribers, they sold the company to
Microsoft for $400 million.

This is a strategy that Steve Jurvetson and Tim Draper,
from the investment firm Draper Fisher Jurvetson, coined as
viral marketing. Since that moment, the firm claims "we won't
consider funding companies whose business plans don't contain at least a germ of the idea, which involves getting your

customers to pass your marketing messages along to friends and associates."[29]

So think of a viral as a strategy and an opportunity to spread your message exponentially, taking advantage of the fact that in the digital world, people are closely connected.

The Viral Opportunities

I once read in the best-selling business book *The Lean Start-Up* that a viral is generated by a feedback loop that can be quantified. The author calls it the "viral loop," and its expansion speed is defined by a mathematical term called the "viral coefficient."[30] It concluded by stating that brands that want to achieve viral growth should be focused on increasing that viral coefficient above anything else.

However, this argument is focused on the wrong part of the viral equation. Contrary to the above claim, companies should not focus on increasing an abstract viral coefficient formula; they should focus on building tangible stuff: products, promotions, content, or events that people are willing to engage with and share.

Here are some proven viral opportunities:

* *Tell a friend*

Encourage your customer to spread the word. Sam Shank, founder of the mobile reservation app Hotel Tonight, saw an opportunity in the travel industry by focusing on the last-minute hotel-booking window. The challenge was that Hotel Tonight had low awareness, a low advertising budget, and low credibility as the app would represent the first automated mobile-only travel agency.

Those limitations triggered an alternative solution, making satisfied customers speak for themselves. The result was the viral platform called "tell a friend." Hotel Tonight gave customers an incentive to share their experiences.

People were already willing to recommend the app to friends; what Hotel Tonight did was to facilitate and accelerate that process. The viral program had motivated users invite friends from the same app by sending them an e-mail or a message through Facebook or Twitter. Then the user would get twenty-five dollars for every new friend that joined. The friend also received the twenty-five-dollar bonus to book the first room.

This is a platform that resembles the one created by Tupperware in the mid-1950s. In the case of Tupperware, it was called the "party plan," a platform that consisted of organizing hosted social events to present plastic-made storage and home products from the Tupperware brand. Any person could become a Tupperware host and organize his or her own product demonstrations. Not only was the salesperson paid for selling but also for the sales made by people he or she recruited. It is what is called "multilevel" marketing, the viral marketing predecessor.

This strategy should not be confused with "frictionless sharing," which, some years ago, many companies adopted to access people's mobile phone contact lists and send them invitations to sign up. This is what the messaging app Spotbros did to increase its user level. You can just imagine that the people who unknowingly sent the branded invitation were not happy at all. Or let's just remember that moment in time when your Facebook friends could see that you were listening to the song "I'm a Barbie Girl" from Aqua thanks to the frictionless strategy initiated by Spotify. Not the right move.

Companies tend to forget that customers are the ones who decide. You have to make them engage with your brand or give them an incentive to participate. In any case, never use something valuable to them without their permission. This is just not starting a long-term relationship off on the right foot.

* *Experience little delights*

What surprising delights could a small brand afford to deliver to their existing customers at basically no cost?

The Washington born fast-casual restaurant chain Sweetgreen leaves gift cards on vehicles that have received a parking ticket to brighten the driver's day with a campaign that they call "random acts of sweetness."

Another random act of kindness that drove sincere social media fan engagement comes from Bill Taylor, cofounder of *Fast Company* magazine. A story about a sick grandmother and a warm bowl of soup from the restaurant chain Panera Bread garnered more than 500,000 likes on Facebook. The story, as told by Taylor,[31] goes like this: after visiting his grandmother in the hospital, Brandon Cook posted the following on his Facebook page:

My grandmother is passing soon with cancer. I visited her the other day and she was telling me about how she really wanted soup, but not hospital soup because she said it tasted "awful." She went on about how she really would like some clam chowder from Panera. Unfortunately Panera only sells clam chowder on Friday. I called the manager Sue and told them the situation. I wasn't looking for anything special, just a bowl of clam chowder. Without hesitation she said absolutely she would make her some clam chowder. When I went to pick it up they wound up giving me a box of cookies as well. It's not that big of a deal to most, but to my grandma it meant a lot. I really want to thank Sue and the rest of the staff from Panera in Nashua, NH, just for making my grandmother happy. Thank you so much!

Panera achieved something that no amount of traditional advertising can buy: a genuine sense of affiliation from people around the world.

It is definitely not a scalable solution, but it does have a huge impact when the story gets covered in the media and shared on social media sites. There are all little human stories that offer big marketing lessons about brands behaving like people rather than faceless companies solely guided by manuals and policies.

Some executives would consider this a costly campaign, but when 75 percent of the orders come from repeat customers, little delights are a wise short-term strategy to generate virality and a long-term strategy to increase loyalty.

*   *Help the product spread*

The product itself can also generate word of mouth and a virality effect. Airbnb is an example to explain how to get virality through your product. The site started to grow faster after adding professional services to show some of houses and allowing unique spaces to rent, even castles and tree houses. Some special rentals were:

–   Eskimo life: Oetz, Austria. Private room in an igloo village. Ice bar nearby. $204/night.
–   Cliffside: Bingin Beach, Bali. Two-story house with maid service. $119/night.
–   Serene room: Habikino, Japan. Surrounded by rice fields and a bamboo forest. $35/night.

What this example shows is that they focused on building products that delivered value that no one had seen before. It was not about capturing the most exquisite travelers; it was about introducing new products that would capture media coverage and achieve social media virality.

At the end of the day, viral strategies are about creating remarkable things that people feel proud of and are passionate about spreading.

If people love it, they will spread it.

3.3. FRAMING

A company should connect its brand to being the leader and creator of a new category that is relevant, new, and exciting to consumers. I call this framing.

Framing is about how people perceive a new category. It is not an internal company exercise; it is about perception. Is a battle between categories rather than a battle between products. It's a different concept than positioning, which establishes how consumers' minds perceive a product compared to that of the competition.

Before the drink Vitamin Water, the beverage industry was framed around taste. Consumers could choose among cola, orange, and lemon sodas. Even as products evolved over time, they only progressed by creating low-calorie and low-sugar versions of their classic flavors. Nothing had really changed.

What Vitamin Water changed was that people could choose a drink based on their moods and energy levels. "Do I feel tired and need an extra energy boost? Or do I want to relax after a tough day at work?" There is a drink for every state of mind. Vitamin Water created a new beverage category, vitamin flavored water, and framed it based on consumers' moods. It is a drink that can adapt to the consumer's lifestyle.

Another example is Salesforce.com. Marc Benioff, founder of Salesforce in 1999, is credited with being the creator of software as a service (SaaS), also known as the cloud computing category. At the time when Benioff launched his product, Microsoft was selling physical software that needed to be installed on computers, customized by a programmer, and paid for maintenance over time—a cost-consuming process that also took significant time to install. It was not an efficient system if you compare it with Benioff's offering. Instead, Salesforce.com customers have no hardware or software to buy, install, maintain, or update. Access to applications is easy: customers just need an Internet connection, and they are ready to go.

The way Salesforce framed this new SaaS category was by using the claims "no software" and "software is obsolete." In relevant industry events and important competitors' conferences, they shouted their framing very loudly and clearly. They hired people who stood outside the building with signs reading "no software" and showing Siebel, one of their competitors, as a biplane and Salesforce.com as a jet fighter. These fake demonstrations were covered by many media channels, including *The Wall Street Journal*. These tactics combined with a bold category framing helped them spread the message.

FRAMING VERSUS POSITIONING

Marketing executives, creative directors, and marketing academics have been talking about brand positioning since the concept started to gain traction in 1972, when Jack Trout and Al Ries wrote a series of articles entitled "The Positioning Era" for *Advertising Age* magazine. It was a concept that was later popularized when they published the book *Positioning— The Battle for Your Mind* (McGraw-Hill, 1981). But positioning only involves managing the consumer's perception of a brand compared to other competing brands. In other words, positioning is about playing the preference game. How can I make my brand preferred over the competitor's?

A small company could compete with a market leader; however, it would not be effective to do it by competing head on. For instance, imagine you are the manager of a small bank called United Jersey Bank, which is based in New York City. It is a bank that operates in the shadows of larger banks with higher presence in the city, such as Citibank or Chase Manhattan. How could Jersey Bank position itself against those big competitors? As Trout and Ries explain in their book, positioning could be approached by identifying the competitors' weaknesses. In this case, a disadvantage for big banks is that large size is closely associated with slow service. So United Jersey Bank can build its positioning strategy around being the fast-moving bank. This is a case of positioning a brand in an existing category.

However, when the brand you launch is intended to create a whole new category, you need to consider framing as a more effective tool. Category framing directly affects how consumers perceive a new offering, and therefore it shapes their attitudes and behaviors toward a new category, not just a product. Based on that, people could immediately reject a new category, or, on the contrary, they could embrace it and become loyal customers.

Here is an example to illustrate this point. Because it is a case that happened centuries ago, it will help us concentrate on the core concept of framing and avoid current socioeconomic and cultural distractions.

One of the most exotic products that arrived from the American colonies was chocolate. Christopher Columbus had already brought cocoa seeds for the Catholic monarchs from the Castile and Aragon regions, which later became Spain. But because they didn't know what to do with them, they probably got forgotten in some corner of the palace. Their flavor was too bitter and spicy, and people would easily get dirty. The new category had not been framed in a way that generated interest.

People had to wait until the sixteenth century, when Hernán Cortés and some Spanish monks who lived in Mexico sent a cocoa shipment to the Barcelona Port, but this time they included a recipe that explained the steps to follow to make hot chocolate. Hot chocolate was a beverage highly valued by the Aztecs at that time. Once in the peninsula, the local monks who received the package prepared the chocolate drink following the new recipe, which allowed them to create the hot chocolate category. Its use became increasingly popular in the following years. Since that moment, chocolate began being framed as a revitalizing and luxurious beverage.

Chocolate soon became a fashionable drink of the nobility, especially as an after-dinner treat. The ladies of the royal class drank this new beverage, sometimes in secret and in small sips. Chocolate was still being mixed with spices at that time, but the framing of how to drink it and the occasion for it had been redefined. From that moment, it only gained more consumer traction. The tipping point arrived when the Spanish church allowed people to drink chocolate without breaking their fasting periods. With such good publicity, this food quickly became a mainstream beverage.

Framing is about making your brand the leader of a new category. A brand is selected not because it is preferred but because the category is preferred and because it is the most relevant brand in the category. Positioning is about winning over another brand within an existing and mature space.

Get the framing right, and the brand will thrive.

LEADING A CATEGORY

As the category creator, you must lead this new category through your brand. If the brand is tightly associated with the new category and you make it grow, your company will benefit from it.

There are two key elements to achieve a leadership position: defining the category and positioning it against the market leader.

1. Define the Category

Defining and promoting a new category has two key advantages:

Newsworthy: A new category is much more newsworthy than just a new business for media to cover as a story. A new category changes consumer habits, can shift markets, and has bigger cultural implications. New businesses, on the other hand, are created every day, and they are usually associated with products.

Credibility: It is more credible to promote a new category than just promoting a new business, which will probably be perceived as an unwanted piece of advertising to sell more.

In any case, the goal will be to create a clear strategic and visual connection between the new category and the brand. Otherwise, all the efforts will be worthless.

The evolution of the rhythm-and-dance video games is a relevant case to demonstrate how to define a category. Video games have always been associated with entertainment but also with young people sitting on sofas for long hours. However, that perception changed with the launch of the Dance Dance Revolution video game, also referred to as DDR. It was a music video game created by Konami and launched in Japan in 1998, and it was released in Europe and the United States one year later in 1999.

People have to stand on an interactive platform, where they step over differently colored arrows that appear on the video screen following the rhythm of the music. It is a mixture of aerobic exercise and entertainment, and it represented a new category in the video-game industry, the rhythm-and-dance category.

So instead of promoting the video game, the company promoted the category as a whole, and it was a success. Media companies started to write about people losing from ten to fifty pounds after playing DDR for hours. Some gamers, like Matthew Keene, even claimed they lost 150 pounds in four months after using DDR periodically.

The media started to cover more similar stories, and the awareness of DDR skyrocketed. Some schools, like the University of Kansas or Caltech, even integrated the DDR game as part of their curricula, giving credit for it. In 2006, Konami announced that DDR games would become part of the 765 state schools in West Virginia in the United States. It was the most credible and newsworthy way for Konami to promote the video game.

2. Position the Small Brand versus the Leader

Apple positioned itself against IBM as a creative and design-oriented solution. The homemade soda brand SodaStream positioned itself as a healthier alternative to Coke or Pepsi. Virgin Airlines positioned itself against British Airways as a more human and service-oriented alternative. Why do small brands tend to do so?

First, it saves you a lot of advertising money: you are taking advantage of the brand awareness of and media interest in these big corporations. So someone who tries to challenge them face to face is a story worth spreading on the news and social media. Second, it helps consumers better understand what the point of difference is of the new category compared to the one to which the big brand belongs and of which they already know.

Frequently, a new category requires further educating the consumer. I am not referring to creating a side-by-side technical comparison between products. This is more about communicating values, about identifying your business as the David versus the Goliath.

The Mexican restaurant chain Chipotle has done exceptionally well at this since its start. When interviewed, Steve Ells, its founder, claimed that he was not following the fast-food rules; he was completely against them. In this industry, with its enormously successful penny-pinching 99 Cents value menu, Ells framed a new category and grew Chipotle by providing flavor from natural meats and fresh vegetables grown "with integrity," as the chain's tagline states. Ells says that fast-food executives thought he was crazy, that he would not be able to play the game by his rules, and that it did not make sense. This is a media story! And this got him lots and lots of media exposure that, at the end of the day, everyone read, and they started to know more about Chipotle's values as a company.

In a second phase, Ells created an emotional and visually unique YouTube story that stressed the differences of his business compared to the traditional fast-food chains. The background song "Back to the Start," sang by Willie Nelson, said it clearly: it was time to go back to the roots, back to being a real farmer and raising animals in a sustainable and caring way. That is framing a category.

Chipotle has successfully led a new category, and at the same time the chain has positioned itself against the big and cold corporations in the fast-food industry.

Create it. Lead it. Own it.

WHAT ARE THE KEYS TO FRAMING?

There are four key elements to consider when framing a new category.

1. Validate

The category's framing must resonate with the user group that the company is targeting. It is all about alignment.

People support ideas that validate their own worldviews. So the brand should not try to insist on changing people's ideas. Instead, it should reinforce them. Row in their direction. Look for a message that your target audience can agree with, and show them how your category and brand can add value to their lives.

The meal kit subscription services category is a great example. Companies like Blue Apron, Plated, and HelloFresh send customers fresh food boxes once a week straight to their doors so that people can cook gourmet meals with a fraction of the effort and benefit from considerable savings.

In fact, one of their biggest selling points is that it beats traditional grocery store shopping when it comes to reducing food waste. As consumers, we can all relate to this idea when we remember finding expired vegetables at the back of the fridge. We bought them at the supermarket, and, weeks later, we end up throwing them out since we bought too many or because we did not come up with any cooking ideas.

From a consumer point of view, it reaffirms that getting the exact portion of vegetables, sauce, and protein to cook will help reduce one's weekly food waste and therefore add up to some savings.

2. Break a Pattern

People react to new and unique things they read or see. This, in fact, is the major key success factor of ideas that spread in any form. People engage with things they have never seen before.

The frame should be unique in its messaging but also in the way it is shown. When Dollar Shave Club, the start-up that delivers shaving razors for a monthly subscription, launched its disruptive service, they created a YouTube video that has gotten fifteen million views to date.

The video not only explained their innovative service but did it in a way that people had never seen before. Instead of producing a predictable commercial, its CEO, Michael Dubin, wrote a unique and funny script that people had never seen before. In the video, Dubin focuses on reinforcing the framing of the new category, which is "smart shaving," which is emphasized by phrases like "Do you like spending twenty dollars a month on brand-name razors? Nineteen dollars go to Roger Federer." But he also introduced shocking language such as "Our blades are f***ing great" and other forms of direct communication that no one would expect from a traditional company.

It is not only about getting the new category framing right; it is also about communicating it in a new and unique way that awakens people's minds.

3. Move

Strong frames are the ones that have an impact on people's emotions, hopefully getting people thrilled to try your product. The frame has to connect at a deeper human level, not only on a rational level.

Chipotle, the Mexican grill chain, created and framed a new category based on the growing interest for slow food, a movement that goes in the opposite direction of traditional fast-food chains. Slow Food is about partnering up with farmers who source plants, seeds, and animals from a local ecosystem, a movement that Chipotle translated into its frame, which is to "serve food with integrity" by finding the best ingredients with respect for the animals, the environment, and the farmers. Since its inception, the company has always promoted its framing rather than its products in articles, on YouTube videos, and in TV ads. That is because Chipotle's role is to act as a new category leader by supporting a food movement, not by playing within an existing category and only claiming how different and cheap its products are. It is all about connecting at an emotional level.

4. Make it Tangible
Frames are mental structures that shape the way we see the world. You can't see touch, see, or hear them.

However, framing can move away from being an abstract concept and become a tangible asset for the brand's benefit. Language plays a key role in activating frames, such as coming up with a concept that people can imagine.

Kraft's DiGiorno frozen pizza introduced a new pizza with a "rising crust" that was not precooked like all the rest in the market. The brand framed it as a frozen pizza with the taste and freshness of a delivery pizza with its tagline "It's not delivery. It's DiGiorno." People can imagine the taste of the freshly cooked crust of a delivery pizza because they have already tried it; it is something tangible.

Frame the category in a way that validates the worldview of your target group of consumers, but present it in a new way that they have never seen before.

FAILURES IN FRAMING

One new category could be framed according to different perspectives, but very few will really generate interest from consumers. A product might represent a significant innovation in the market; however, whether the consumer will accept or reject it depends on how it is framed.

In 2007, Danone launched a brand-new product called Essensis in France, Spain, and Italy. In a few words, they tried to introduce edible cosmetics in the Mediterranean region. In those markets, it represented the first product that promised to improve skin quality and wrinkles, and it created a category called "nutricosmetique." The category already existed in other countries like Japan, where a consumer can buy soda drinks with collagen that renovate the skin from within.

The problem was that Danone framed the category in a way that people didn't believe or validate. Danone had been selling very successful products such as Actimel, with bifidus bacteria, and Danacol, which helped reduce people's cholesterol levels. It made sense to consumers that those products enhanced people's health. But how could a yogurt smooth your wrinkles and give you shiny skin? Was it too far out? Furthermore, would that mean that consumers might be eating some hydrating cream?

Even with the huge advertising investment surrounding its launch, which was around 9.3 million euros in France alone, the category failed. Sales never took off, and they even declined with each month that passed. Consequently, Danone removed the products from all markets, making it one of its biggest failures from the last years. People didn't validate the idea that a yogurt could become a beauty product.

Validate frameworks with your local customers.

REFRAMING

Procter & Gamble created the "household odor eliminator" category when, in 1998, they launched Febreze. It was an excellent product to remove odors from fabrics, especially from sofas. In 2011, the product had achieved significant business with $140 million in sales. However, because people did not use the product on many occasions, it was stuck on supermarket shelves for months before a consumer decided to do a repurchase.

So the company dug deeper to understand exactly how the heavy users used the product. The findings showed that people were using the spray all over the place, not just on clothes and furniture. The solution was clear: P&G reframed the category and the Febreze brand into a freshener spray that could also remove odors from fabrics. Their new framing became "a breath of fresh air." Three years later, Febreze had become a $750 million brand in the United States.

Reframing should not only be considered for turning around negative sales or low adoption rates, but it should also be strongly regarded as a way to move a brand from a niche market to a mainstream market.

Elevate your brand by redefining it.

3.4. THE LAUNCH PHASES
THIS IS NOT HOLLYWOOD

The launch process is a critical area for any new venture. However, media and marketing books have given an over-importance to the first days and weeks of the business launch. New businesses should not follow the Hollywood industry, where films are promoted intensively weeks before so that the opening weekend captures as much money as possible. At the end of the day, a movie will get kicked out of the cinemas if it doesn't make a decent box-office opening. Furthermore, the movie industry is structured by time windows, so there is more time pressure to get the expected financial results. It has to generate sales quickly because sooner or later it will be removed and released on DVD, video on demand, and so on.

New ventures do not work this way. A new company must gain traction, and usually the process tends to adopt a slower pace. Mass takes time to build. Therefore, you shouldn't be misguided and focus too much on the first weeks' sales because if you don't achieve the expected sales, you will probably change your strategy and product and ultimately sabotage your real goal, which is to grow a business.

The media often describes business stories as overnight successes; in reality, it takes time to create momentum, build a customer baseline, and find the right product mix and effective promotional vehicles. There is an example that shows this growing, steady, but slow adoption. Guitar Hero, one of the best-selling video games in history, did not generate massive interest in the first weeks it appeared on the market. Guitar Hero was selling more every single month during its first year on the market. It was a growing curve. Instead, most video-game launches have an opposite declining curve like in the Hollywood industry. During the first month, sales peak, and from that point on, every month the video game sells half of what it did the previous month.

A similar case happened to the novel *50 Shades of Grey*. Not so long ago, millions of people around the world were reading it. What you probably don't know is that this novel was launched as a self-published e-book. Now, not many people read the novel during this early stage. Most people waited until they saw it on the best-sellers list, and other people waited for a friend's recommendation. But the book gained traction, and with time it generated positive word of mouth that drove more readers to buy the novel.

For this reason, we need to understand that the traditional launch process of big corporations cannot be taken into account when creating a new product or service that changes the rules—especially because consumers have to see if your product generates a unique new value to them before they can recommend it and spread the word. You cannot pressure consumers to adopt it faster, the same way you cannot throw money at the adoption curve, because it won't make a difference.

Early wins can help get the brand off to a good start, but they are not enough. You must also plan for long-term success.

WHEN BIG ADVERTISING BUDGETS WON'T MAKE ANY DIFFERENCE

Great companies don't throw money at
problems; they throw ideas at problems.

—Greg McAdoo, venture capitalist
and partner at Sequoia Capital

Millions of people like to drink fresh orange juice when they wake up in the morning. So just imagine the size of the opportunity. The orange production for 2016 is estimated at 47.9 million tons worldwide[32]. Now take into account that there are two global leaders in this category—Tropicana and Minute Maid—and there is also significant participation from private-label brands nearly matching the leaders' quality. It is a big opportunity but a highly competitive and dangerous field to enter.

Will big advertising bucks buy your company a place in this category? Can you just rely on launching a regular orange juice and back it up with $100 million in investment? Or would you approach this situation by creating a new category that would attract fresh-orange-juice consumers to your new brand?

In this case, there is the P&G way and the Innocent way. In 1982, P&G launched a new orange-juice brand named Citrus Hills Fresh Select with a $100 million advertising budget. As in the previous cases I have described in this book, the two incumbents, Tropicana and Minute Maid, reacted with a twofold strategy. First, they immediately increased their promotional budgets to silence Citrus Hills Fresh Select's market impact. Second, Coca-Cola alerted the US Food and Drug Administration that P&G had to remove its "fresh" claim from its label. P&G´s "fresh" juice was in fact not as fresh as you would expect. On the label, there was a small disclaimer stating that it was "fresh from concentrate," not quite a transparent and fair practice to consumers. The FDA classified it as false advertising, and in less than twenty-four hours this story became the headline of every national newspaper and television broadcast, consequently impacting its consumer credibility and the company's ability to promote the juice as freshly made.

P&G learned the hard way that big advertising budgets won't make a dent in a market unless you introduce a new, unique, and relevant solution that a consumer values.

On the other side of the coin, there is Innocent Drinks, a company that successfully entered the bottled-juice category without having $100 million in advertising.

Innocent Drinks is the classic lemonade stand turned into a multi-million-dollar company. It reinvented fresh juice. Some people say they invented the smoothies category; however, as I have been saying throughout the book, concepts are never invented. Instead, they are an evolution. Another company named Pete and Johnny (also known as PJs) was already selling bottled smoothies in the country. What Innocent did differently was to offer pure, fresh, and all-natural smoothies, not from concentrate. Innocent succeeded where P&G failed: making fruit fun while being healthy.

Was this luck? The same approach was used in 1980 and 1983 by two juice companies that were born in California— Odwalla Juices and Naked Juices respectively—just at the same time when P&G launched its new Citrus Hills brand. Instead of entering the market the P&G way, they built their brands by offering freshly made juice. Their products and brands were so successful that twenty years later, both companies were acquired by Coca-Cola and Pepsi respectively.

Big advertising budgets are meant for maintaining brands in the minds of consumers, not for building businesses. So focus on creating a new and unique product that can be framed in a new category, and introduce it as a reinvention. Then build awareness and credibility through word of mouth, social media, PR, and grassroots marketing. These are by far more effective strategies to sustainably grow a business and a brand.

Never underestimate the underdog.

THE FIVE LAUNCH PHASES

In the quest for the quick hit, the easy and common way to start a business is to focus only on the launching date. However, an overambitious, winner-take-all attitude at that point in time could lead to financial difficulties and even bankruptcy. After all, when someone's read or seen something about your brand just once, they're not likely to actually buy it. There's so much clutter and so many new products to choose from that any launch requires time and a planning process to make a dent.

The hard part is to build a strategic pipeline of news and events that engages with a growing community of consumers and that allows the business to be scaled and reach a main-stream status.

Let's consider each phase in more detail.

1. Test

Test the product prototype, the beta version of your service, with a small and local group of people who have a high interest in your project. By small, I mean a handful of people whom you can have direct access to receive their candid feedback fast and cheaply. Your goal should be to improve or even rethink your solution before launching it.

In 1999, a new type of grocery store was born, the online supermarket. The company that led the subcategory was Webvan. However, in 2001, the dot-com venture was in a deep downfall precipitated by an excess of ambition. Instead of testing its model in one city to learn from its mistakes and then expanding its improved business model to more cities, Webvan preferred to launch nationally. So all their mistakes were the same in all the different cities where they were present. Furthermore, Webvan spent $45 million building facilities in New York, Baltimore, and Seattle for operations that never took off. In total, the company was able to get $1 billion in funding, which could not compensate for their mistakes and low sales volume.

Many companies have the ambition to get bigger, to grow their sales at a fast pace, but what you cannot ignore as a marketer is that it takes time to create a solid customer base and to change behaviors. So ignoring the testing phase can be a critical mistake for a new business.

In this stage, you should validate and fine tune your business model and products in a cheap and fast way, not in a blockbuster approach like Webvan did.

Remember Webvan. Especially because nobody else does.

2. Prelaunch

Common sense might tell you to promote your product when it's ready to sell. The truth is that you don't need to wait until you have the product finished to start promoting your business.

The prelaunch phase is about generating excitement. Therefore, it is the best moment in time to build buzz by showing previews of your product through videos, articles, and exclusive events. In other words, create content and exclusive consumer experiences that will generate word of mouth among people who share the same passion.

The goal is to get media professionals and early adopters to listen to your story and generate interest so that they share it with their contacts.

Exclusivity can be key. When Spotify built its beta version website in the United States, the company sent limited invitations to try the new service. Again, this is a great way to control demand for operational purposes, build buzz in the country, and gradually build a solid customer baseline that benefits from the best possible customer service. The invite-only strategy became the hottest thing to get. However, months after the Spotify launch, they decided to open the doors to everyone. The only condition was to have a Facebook account to sign in on for six months of access to millions of songs.

Exclusivity is a proven strategy for the prelaunch phase. Exclusivity allows a company to:

* Test its product before the official launch
* Ensure that only a limited number of consumers are affected by problems
* Adjust the operations or systems, which could not be robust enough at the beginning
* Generate interest among the general public
* Steadily grow the consumer base up without compromising operations and service due to potential high volumes of traffic

There are many marketing cases that support the exclusivity strategy, both in the online and offline worlds. So it is something definitely worth considering and is proven to deliver strong results across different industries.

Generate hype on the launching phase, but put more attention into the following stages.

3. The After Launch

As I mentioned, the launching date of a business is not the only event an entrepreneur should be focusing on. The after launch will be as important as the announcement day.

Generating buzz around a new product is easy. You have media interested in your concept, passionate people willing to sign up to be the first to review it, and readers ready to know more about it. However, sustaining the buzz is the big challenge. You just have to think how many new ventures you have seen this year. You will probably remember a viral video that people were talking about one week, but now it seems to have disappeared. For that reason, you need people and customers to keep talking. You have to think about growing your promotional efforts over time.

You can do so by making major announcements during the following weeks. It could be a partnership that excites potential customers, or it could be unveiling a product feature to explain how unique the product is. In any case, make sure you have something in your pipeline to replicate the initial spark that you generated at the launch to create a second and third firestorm.

> *Be creative. Innovate consistently on the little things that the big companies ignore. Little things often make big differences in business.*
>
> —RICHARD BRANSON, FOUNDER
> OF VIRGIN GROUP

4. Community

Marketing books and professionals tend to use the word "target" to refer to the end consumer that will buy their products. The problem is that this word is very dangerous. For instance, you could think that a target group for a new beer brand could be defined as people between twenty-five and thirty-five years old, males, who obviously like beer. Is this enough data to build a relevant brand for them? It doesn't even scratch the surface of their interests. That is why we have to forget about using the word "target."

New ventures should only care about communities—in other words, a group of people who are tightly connected by shared interests and location. The brand vision, and consequently the promotional campaigns, you want to define is built around their passions and interests. And you want to do it on a local level to get a real interaction between the brand and people. Yes, even in the digital age, local is still key for a company to gain traction.

Who won in the online marketplace that outsourced jobs to neighbors? TaskRabbit.com, who began a city-by-city launch strategy? Or Zaarly.com, which launched its start-up on a national scale from day one? TaskRabbit won over Zaarly with its local and sequential approach. Why? Because group relationships are critical in the adoption or rejection of an innovation.

It is like setting a fire. The most valuable piece at the campsite is the small and dry branch to start a fire. So if your product or service is not spreading, it might be because you are focusing on too many people, and you are not directing your message and idea to an interested community of people. In other words, the people you are addressing are not closely connected. When you connect with a smaller and concentrated group of people, it is far easier to spread your message.

Without kindling, without a community, you will not be able to set a fire.

4.1. Community: Find a Niche Community
Building a brand around a community is a proven way to start a new business from scratch. There are two main benefits to support this strategy:

A. Relevancy
Communities are better connected because they share a common interest. So talking about a new product that improves their lives is something that they would naturally do. Then when the other people from the tribe are exposed to that new concept, they will probably get interested and will like to know a little bit more and even consider buying it because it will also probably make their lives easier.

The closer you connect and interact with a community, the more they will see your brand as being relevant.

B. Cost
Communication with small groups of people is far more cost-effective than targeting a larger market. A larger market that includes people completely out of sync with your ideas and values won't consider buying your brand, so why would it make sense to focus on them?

Furthermore, the larger the market, the more money you will need to reach them. Larger events, national media channels—it is a waste of money at this stage.

There is a case that clearly explains the difference between engaging with a community and communicating in one direction to the general public. This is the story of two companies: Gatorade, the sports drink that was born to improve the

University of Florida football team's performance, and Isotop, which tried to sell a sports drink with "fresher" vitamins to every person who practices sports.

On one side, there is the successful business case of Gatorade, the refreshing and isotonic drink that created the sports drink category in the mid-'60s. Everything begins because there is a consumer problem to solve. And this case is no different. In this case, football players from the University of Florida, the Florida Gators, lost so much weight during games and training sessions that they didn't have any fluids left to urinate. So Dewayne Douglas, assistant coach for the Florida Gators, contacted the University of Florida's kidney disease specialist, Robert Cade, about what could be causing this situation.

Cade and his peer researchers speculated that electrolytes, mainly sodium and potassium, were being lost through their sweat. The hot weather and the high levels of physical exercise combined were damaging the players' performance. So Cade proposed to their head coach, Ray Graves, to do a test with some players. The results were immediately visible. Body salts were out of balance, blood sugar was low, and their blood levels were way too low.

So Cade and his peer researchers quickly formulated a drink that would replace those minerals lost in sweat. The first version of the drink was simply a combination of water, sodium, sugar, potassium, phosphate, and lemon juice. The players from the University of Florida tested this new beverage in the 1965 games. The results were so successful that some credited their first Orange Bowl victory to their new isotonic drink. The story started to spread around the community, and their new secret weapon became something that interested other football professionals and coaches.

Shortly after their win, in 1967, researchers from the University of Florida College of Medicine, led by Robert Cade, closed an agreement with Stokely-Van-Camp, Inc., a canned-food packaging company, to produce and distribute Gatorade as a commercial product in the United States. The company made a commitment to the football community that, later that year, they would sponsor the National Football League, which was the first-ever sponsorship for the brand.

The company continued rowing with the same strategy of focusing on the football community until, in 1983, the Quaker Oats Company purchased Gatorade for $220 million. The company expanded the distribution of the brand on a national level but also into Canada, South America, Australia, and some parts of Europe and Asia in the following decade.

The key aspect of this case is the importance of not only designing but also growing and promoting the product within a small community in order to gain traction, credibility, and word of mouth.

On the other side of the coin is a company called Isotop. It didn't create any subcategory but positioned itself as the promoter of a new sports drink with the additional benefit of electrolytes blending with the water when you turned the cap, apparently keeping those vitamins and minerals active for when you really needed them.

First, there was no previous traction of consumers looking for "fresher" mineral salts. This was only a benefit that the company assumed people would look for, and, in fact, they didn't. Second, the company sold its product directly to the mass market. Consumers could find Isotop in big supermarkets and other large-sized stores. But it lost the relevancy battle. It was not even relevant to any sports community. Besides, the costs of building such an ambitious project also required huge sales pressure from day one. For that reason, it is so important to follow a community strategy to launch a new product. It makes sense in terms of investment because you can just create a small batch for a small number of people. Then grow from there. And it makes sense to connect your brand with a small community because it accelerates brand visibility and word of mouth within the tribe.

That is what Clif Bar did when it launched its business—and it still does it. Clif Bar went up against some of the world's largest food companies, especially Nestlé, which sells the PowerBar and which created the sports bar category in the late 1980s.

Clif Bar focused on selling its good-tasting bars at seven hundred bike stores, given that its founder, Gary Erickson, was a cycling fan himself. He understood that the product was designed for people like him: the biker who did not enjoy eating those bland and chewy bars that competitors sold at that time.

On top of that, Erickson launched a highly local strategy around the cycling community. He sponsored existing local events and even created new ones like the Epiphany ride, where Clif Bar employees get together and try to get as many people with the same passion to ride. There, Erickson could interact with other cyclists and let them try the product using sampling stations—because the company's vision is not only to sell bars but to ignite and inspire cyclists. What Clif Bar did distinctively was to be closer with their target community than their competitors were.

Tribes are what matter.

4.2. Community: Building One Customer Segment at a Time

Great companies are built, not launched. This growth strategy of building market share over time from customer segment to customer segment has delivered results for the vast majority of small brands showcased: Gatorade, Nike, Red Bull, Zaarly.com, and Facebook, for instance. This strategy reduces the financial risk as it allows you to slowly build up expenses, which can be covered with the increasing revenues.

However, other businesses might not find it adequate, especially in the digital world, where you cannot apply the same cost rationale. On top of that, some new ventures need to rapidly grow to avoid getting copied. Clones can quickly appear with an even bigger marketing budget coming from a venture capital firm.

In other cases, companies' success directly depends on the number of users that will use their service. Volume is essential to grow. For instance, WhatsApp needed to capture the mainstream market so that their messaging system added value to the end user. It just wouldn't make sense to text people using different messaging apps. The company that got the most people to use their messaging platform fastest won.

Jeff Bezos, who launched Amazon in 1994, knew that the key to success would be to sell books and CDs all over the country and the world. After the second month in business, Amazon.com was selling to all fifty states in the United States and to over forty-five countries.

The problem comes with companies that want to grow fast because they have set too-high expectations in terms of speed of growth and total sales. Take Segway, the two-wheeled self-balancing electric vehicle. Steve Jobs predicted that it would impact the world the same way the personal computer did. However, when it was introduced in 2001, it was perceived as a big failure by the technology industry. The production was set at around fifty thousand units a year, but the actual sales for the first seven years were below thirty thousand units.

Why did it go wrong? Apparently, Segway did a lot of things right. Its technical innovations were protected by patents to avoid copies. The product works flawlessly. Since the day of its launch, it got worldwide media coverage. It was one of the most visible products of its time. Even George W. Bush famously took a tumble while trying out a Segway in Maine.

The fatal mistake was not focusing on building the brand first within a community or a group of consumers. The average consumer wouldn't be able to spend $3,000 just to move short distances. Furthermore, people need time to change traditional behaviors such as walking or riding a bicycle. And to make matters worse, Segway didn't provide any support on their distribution channels. They just assumed that people would learn by themselves. In fact, they decided to sell it on Amazon. This is not a new electric toothbrush that comes in a small box and that, in order to make it work, you just need to press "on." So why try to sell them this electric vehicle that creates so many questions and uncertainties?

Yet within the professional segments, Segway was received with special interest, and sales quickly took off. As I previously explained, you have to design and market to the extremes, to the group of people who will truly value the benefits of your product. In this case, it was an optimal transportation system for the hospitality, logistics, and retail industries. There is a real benefit to decreasing an employee's walking distance, reducing fatigue, and improving maneuverability through warehouses without heavy maintenance and with no fuel required.

If Segway had begun its launch strategy focusing on these high usage groups first, it would have been a way far more profitable way to grow. Throughout this time, the company would have steadily increased its visibility among the consumer market to further explore its interest.

Make a difference to one customer segment at a time.

4.3. Community: Promote a Hit Single

Elmo is not just a puppet. The ticklish red monster pays the bills for most of Sesame Street. He is the undisputed ambassador of the brand from over one hundred different Muppets that the show hosts. So it is no surprise that he also leads the top of the list of the TV show merchandise. In 1996, when they made the Tickle Me Elmo vibrating and giggling toy, the demand for it was so unexpectedly high that it disappeared from store shelves in the blink of an eye. "Elmo mania" even caused some physical injuries to a clerk from a Wal-Mart store when a crowd spotted him placing Elmos down the aisle. The employee was literally stampeded and suffered injuries to his back, a broken rib, and a concussion. You could even find the toy selling for $1,500 in newspaper classifieds and on the Internet.[33]

What has Elmo got to do with marketing and launching a new venture? Every company has its own Elmo. Every company has a hero product. And a marketer's job consists of identifying the product with the greatest potential and using it to promote the business as a whole. If you focus all your efforts on one product, you will be able to build more awareness than you would by investing in three or four different products and you will capitalize on word of mouth at the same time.

This happens in every industry. You are driving down the road, and you hear a song that you like for the first time, but you didn't get the name of the artist. The next day you hear it again; perhaps you are even able to Shazam it, or you pay attention when the DJ says the name of the song. Two days later, you hear it again. Then one day, you buy the single. Do you stop there? No. You also want to listen to the other songs on the album, and you end up buying two more tunes that you really like.

Products are like singles. First, you have to identify the one with most appeal, the one with most potential. Next, you have to commit to promote it in a way that not only drives product sales but also generates awareness of your business and all the other solutions you offer.

Say one thing. Repeat.

4.4. Community: Nobody Buys a Product the First Time

One of the most frequent comments that I hear from entrepreneurs, especially from start-up founders, is "We have a significant number of registered users; however, only ten percent of them buy our product or subscribe to our service."

How many times you have seen an ad on YouTube, on a magazine, or even on TV that grabbed your attention? Now, how many of these products have you actually bought? A fraction?

We live in a moment in time when we get hit by advertising thousands of times a day. It is believed that a consumer could see around three thousand advertising messages a day. That includes product packaging in the aisle of a supermarket, delivery trucks, billboards, mobile ads, TV, and window displays, just to name a few.

The key is not to impact once; make people register, and then claim you have increased your user base by 500 percent. The key is to create a customer, to generate a sale, and to establish a long-term relationship.

For that purpose, more than a single brand impact is needed. The first time, a person might think, *That's a cool product; that could be useful.* The second time, he or she might say, "I should remember to check it out." Then the third time he or she sees it, the person might buy it.

So in order for a person to become aware of a new product, repetition is needed. The group of people a company is targeting should have seen your product several times (frequency) and in different media channels that they consume. For instance, it could be word of mouth, a magazine article, or even a sponsored local event. All of those impacts should deliver on three brand attributes: how credible, how relevant, and how energetic the brand promise is to the consumer.

Credibility is needed because a small brand needs to establish trust in order to acquire new customers. A brand has to focus on promoting messages that are trustworthy, and advertising cannot do that. Therefore, the company should concentrate on alternative tactics such as sharing customers' reviews and journalists' articles and connecting with consumers through organizing fun and valuable local events.

Relevancy is necessary because people need to understand the uniqueness of the added value of your product. And energy is required because the brand needs to feel like an exciting proposal not only because it is offering an innovative product, but also because it has a magnetic personality that attracts people who want to get involved with it. For example, Taylor Made representatives travel to golf clubs to demonstrate their products and bring to life an enjoyable brand experience. The restaurant chain Denny's gave away more than two million breakfasts in one day to capture new customers. Or another example is Apple, which has built huge events in their retail stores for each of their product launches that led to thousands of people queuing up and global media covering what can be called a perfect brand ceremony.

Break through the selective attention filter through brand credibility, brand relevancy, and brand energy.

Starts Are Slow Because They Require New Behaviors
Building critical mass is a slow process. There is always a social stigma around new categories that make people do things

differently. For instance, Airbnb, the online apartment-rental site, demanded a brand-new mind-set. People can think, *Why should I go to someone else's house and sleep in their bed?* or *Is it really worth it to rent my apartment to a complete stranger?* Even governments are against the new disruptors. Look at what happened to the mobile-based taxi services such as Uber. For the last few years, taxi associations have been demonstrating against this service in Paris, London, New York, and Barcelona.

Reinventors are game changers. So it is critical to understand that game-changing businesses will require new behaviors that take time to get adopted. Therefore, the team leader needs to manage the team's and the stakeholder's short-term expectations and strategically plan accordingly, especially from a financial point of view.

If you start a business, which will require a significant degree of marketing investment and consumer education, you will probably need to secure additional financial backing upfront to overcome those challenges. You will need to spread the capital mindfully throughout the course of months and not throw everything away during the first weeks of the launch of the company.

Consumer education is not cheap, and it takes time. Plan accordingly.

4.5. Community: Focus on Winning Locally

If you were to open a new ice-cream shop, you would probably start by following common sense, which would be to find the warmest and sunniest cities. At the end of the day, people tend to eat more ice cream where there is sunny weather. For instance, the cities that consume the most ice cream in the United States are Long Beach, California, and Dallas, Texas, two cities in the south with warm climates.

However, isn't this too obvious? As an entrepreneur, are you really sure you would want to go to any of these cities with hundreds of competitors? Yes, there is a high ice-cream consumption per capita, but is this really key to your business? Not at all.

Play where there are no competitors. Ben & Jerry's, the ice-cream-maker duo, took this approach. How about targeting a city with college students and with no ice-cream shops?

The duo started their business and learned the art of ice-cream making through a distance-learning course. So they thought they would be much better off in a place with no competition since they had no idea what were they doing. Ben thought of Burlington, Vermont, not the warmest place in the country. It is only forty-two miles from Canada, but there it is a college town with thousands of students and, better yet, no ice-cream parlor. Since the opening day, their first store was a huge success, and everyone knows the rest of the story. Ben & Jerry's built an ice-cream empire by starting off in an uncommon place.

Focus on winning locally before you move to the next city or to the next customer segment.

In a second phase, adopting a city-by-city approach will build brand visibility and generate energy within a specific region. Starbucks is one of the companies that has supported this strategy. Rather than spread investment across a whole country, the coffee company found success by deeply developing its brand in a specific city before jumping to new one. City shares matter. But as you might think, there is a threat with this approach; a company leaves space for other new players to enter the market. But in a retail environment, this risk will always be present. If a competitor does not copy your business in the same city, it will appear in another state or in another country.

It happens in the digital world. Even if you think you can just create the same e-commerce site in all the languages of the world to build a barrier against competitors, a local competitor will still appear that will better adapt their offering to consumers and beat you in that city, state, or country. Uber, the private taxi app, has many clones around the globe. In Mexico, the United Kingdom, and Spain, there are local players outcompeting them. But that does not mean they have to lose focus on their main market, the United States. That would thinly reduce their resources and budget, and they would end up winning nowhere.

In 1970, a young entrepreneur called Paul Orfalea started a small copy shop in Santa Barbara next to a hamburger stand. It was named Kinko's after the nickname that college friends gave him because of his kinky hair. By 2004, there were more than 1,200 Kinko's around the world, a business empire in capital letters.

Now remember that personal computers weren't developed until the late '70s and the beginnings of the 1980s, and the photocopying business was in its first stages of significant growth. However, there were already businesses providing photocopying services around the United States, and he knew he didn't want to compete with them. For that reason, he opened his first copy shop in a place where there was a great need, next to the University of Santa Barbara, and yet there was no business offering this service.

Orfalea mentions that the place was so small that when they needed a second copy machine, they had to lug it out onto the sidewalk. That is what I call starting small but being very focused on offering something new without competitors around.

The best strategy in war is to
win without a fight.

—Sun Tzu

4.6. Community: Build an Engaged Community
Building your business around a community is key in order to grow, but can any company win this game?

Only companies that are truly committed to a group of people will win. Only authentic brands. A brand has to generate true value for consumers. It won't gain credibility by creating TV ads, billboards, and nice printed graphics in magazines, as the following example shows.

The skateboarding category had been led and created by the iconic brand Powell Peralta. The company was founded by George Powell, a Stanford University engineer who worked in the aerospace industry, and by Stacy Peralta, a skateboarder who built the Bones Brigade team. Their business was based on a new technology, the urethane wheels that improved the ride on skateboards by making them run smoothly, as well as by introducing new materials like aluminum and fiberglass to produce their unique decks. Powell brought in the technology. Peralta built the most iconic skateboard team of all time: Steve Caballero, Tony Hawk, Tommy Guerrero, Lance Mountain, Rodney Mullen, and Mike McGill.

But this could not have happened if it had not been for the Powell Peralta financial support, especially thanks to Stacy Peralta, who acted as a mentor for each of the members. The brand blended perfectly with that team to help them become the best skaters of the decade. Those kids invented all the modern skateboard maneuvers.

Were they the best at that time? Not at all. Small brands cannot afford to pay the top sports celebrities, but, more importantly, it wouldn't fit the brand. An underdog brand needs to be good at identifying talent and growing together at the same time. It supports the brand value and also the financials.

So Peralta initiated his journey to find those exceptional kids with the highest potential who were still under the radar. He looked for attitude, for looks of disappointment when they lost, for kids who had fire in them. Once Peralta built the team, he needed to create a higher purpose for them. What do these young newcomers stand for? And how will they connect with the brand?

At that time, skateboarding ads were generic and boring, which definitely didn't reflect the values of true skateboarding—the sense of being free, to invent new tricks, to defy the established: a new lifestyle itself. Peralta hired the photographer Craig Stecyk to help him illustrate this new group.

Pictures that would act as free content were sent to magazines to promote the Bones Brigade, the new rebels of skateboarding. Not even a single picture of a skateboard was shown in those pictures. They only showed an attitude, a new lifestyle.

But what Powell Peralta didn't expect is that this new category would become a downward trend. By the early 1980s, skateboarding began a deep decline: skate parks closed, magazines stop publishing, talented skaters quit, and no sponsors wanted to get into that market. No one trusted skateboarding except Powell Peralta. And because several magazines closed and media publishers were not interested in covering this topic, the brand decided to create their path.

In 1982, they created their first feature-length movie called *Skateboarding in the Eighties*, a video that began gaining public attention and fans around the Bones Brigade group. Following its success, they continued this strategy, creating and distributing their own skateboarding videos. In 1985, they released *Future Primitive* and, in 1987, *The Search for Animal Chin*.

Powell Peralta created video manifestos. They pioneered the art of content marketing in those early years the same way that Red Bull now dominates digital content supporting extreme and action sports. The Bones Brigade became like rock stars. They were flying all over the world, from Australia to Japan. They were even invited to a castle to meet George Harrison's son.

This journey would not have been possible without the continuous support that Powell Peralta gave to those promising kids. The company was paying them per board sold. So, when they started off, they were earning eighty-five cents a month. By the late 1980s, they were earning $20,000 and also opening their doors to successful long-term sports careers that grew exponentially with time, when the sport got more popular.

Nike, meanwhile, was watching this trend from the outside, thinking how it could get a piece of this growing market share. It was not until 1997 that Nike launched its skate shoes to compete against native brands such as DC shoes, Emerica, and Vans. However, the attempt was not working. Nike didn't have the endorsement of top skaters and lacked the credibility since it sold the shoes in traditional sports stores, not in specialist skate shops. After all its investments, it was not able to build a community of Nike skateboarders. So, after five years implementing this strategy, it realized that it had to follow the path of other successful brands in the space.

The result was that in 2002, it launched a new brand called Nike Skateboard (Nike SB), taking advantage of their "zoom air technology" used in basketball shoes. But still the new brand didn't take off. It was not until 2004 that Nike started to sign skate stars who endorsed their shoes: Paul Rodriguez, Lewis Marnell, and even Lance Mountain from Powell Peralta. In the end, the giant had to follow the steps of the respected small brands to at least be present in the skateboard market and grow organically from there.

For this reason, authenticity is key to engage with a community. It is not about creating cool skateboarding ads. It is something a brand needs to earn over time as a consequence of having a strong brand vision and being loyal and authentic to it—an attribute that needs to come from two places.

First, it comes from adding real value to customers, in this case by offering innovative and the best-performing skateboarding products in the market. Second, it comes from helping communicate people's personalities, ideas, and lifestyles and putting them together in an exclusive tribe. Brands can also be considered an extension of an individual, especially in this sport. In the skate world, people wouldn't like to be seen as inauthentic. They want to wear, eat, drink, and live the brands that firmly commit to their sport, not brands that are clearly seen an opportunists.

Avoid cutting corners. Build an authentic community over time.

5. Mainstream

One of the biggest challenges for a small brand and reinventor that already leads a niche market is whether its business can be scaled without losing what made it so special as it goes mainstream. Some brands have been very successful at it, such as Nike, Aquarius, and Red Bull. Others have tried it and failed, like what happened to the shoe brand Vans.

So what makes a company successful when scaling? The key factor is to identify the set of brand benefits that existing customers value in order to keep them and that also will attract a broader audience and therefore gain more reach.

There are two sets of strategies to broaden the audience. On one hand, a company could look into another profitable synergic market like Nike did when it got into the basketball business after succeeding in the running category. It was a strategy that made sense for Nike given that each sport required different equipment and a different spokesperson to generate credibility and awareness.

On the other hand, a company could jump directly from a niche market to the mainstream market like Red Bull did by moving from a single and polarizing flavor to a new fruit-flavored line and by making its brand presence more global and ubiquitous through sponsoring action-sports events with international awareness and distributing videos of them through social media and TV networks.

In any case, there is one challenge that will be critical: to identify the key brand attributes and the products that will maintain a business's current customer base to fund the growth process and that will be compelling enough to attract new customers.

An excellent case from which we can extract valuable lessons and that will guide us through the expansion process is the evolution of the brand Aquarius, which moved from a sports drink to a mass-market beverage.

Aquarius is a sports drink that was launched in 1992 in Spain by Coca-Cola, taking advantage of the Barcelona Olympic Games that were going to take place that summer. It was a good opportunity to build a brand by associating it with all the positive attributes and credibility of the Olympic Games. Besides, it was a tactical move to block any competitor like Isostar from gaining market share, thus making it irrelevant.

Aquarius was launched in two flavors: orange and lemon. The product was clearly positioned for the sports- and health-conscious consumer. However, over the next year, the small brand started climbing uphill and being noticed more by the general public. So Coca-Cola saw the potential to reposition the brand and reframe the category for the mass market. Starting from 1993, they began a new strategy to break into the mainstream market. The Coca-Cola marketing executives changed three things: the framing, the packaging, and the communication.

1. Framing
They identified an Aquarius attribute that was relevant and credible for existing customers and for the general public: "Life is a very tough sport," translated from the Spanish slogan "La vida es un deporte muy duro." At that time, it highly resonated with the early 1990s culture, when executives aspired to become Wall Street investors or ambitious businessmen like in the *The Bonfire of the Vanities*, which was released in the same decade. By doing that, they would also create a new category, which would be the "sports drink for everyday use."

2. Packaging
Sports drinks have always been associated with five-hundred-milliliter plastic bottles that are shaped to be easily grabbed with one hand, a design to better suit the athlete who will carry it away to go running or work out around the gym.

However, Aquarius reframed the market with a new approach. Instead of using the slim-shaped sports bottle, they launched the drink using a 330-milliliter aluminum can, the standard can size that any soft drink brand uses, from Coca-Cola to Sprite. That small change probably had the biggest impact on transforming Aquarius into an increasingly popular drink within the general market. Consumers saw the sports drink as a refreshing beverage. The consumer framework led them to associate Aquarius with being an everyday refresher.

So what the Aquarius executives did was to push this association further. They created a plastic bottle for the instant and differed everyday consumption and increased its distribution into the traditional mass-market channels: vending machines, supermarkets, and also small shops. Now everyone could access the product. This trend continued to evolve in the following years, when a short-necked glass bottle was also introduced for the hotel, restaurant, and catering sector.

3. Communication
A new TV campaign was created to guarantee nationwide visibility of the repositioned product. The ad showed an athlete and a businessman side by side overcoming different challenges at the same time. The voiceover narrated the following:

"What is tougher for you, sport or life? A hundred-meter race or going to work? The three thousand hurdles or a traffic jam? The gym or the weekly shopping? A race against the clock or racing all day against time? Aquarius helps you restore the essential minerals and fluids that you lose in sport and in life. Aquarius. Life is a very tough sport."

Results
The new strategy went live with the airing of the previously described TV spot in 1993. Sales increased around 40 to 50 percent throughout the following eight years. Even during

2002 and 2003, sales steadily grew, even though they grew at an inferior rate than during the launch, when the brand had no advertising support at all. The brand had flawlessly been adopted by the Spanish general consumers thanks to the repositioning of the brand and by reframing the category.

Humans are extraordinary, aren't they? This is what the Coca-Cola executives thought about this brand evolution, to the extent that they created a new TV campaign after the slogan "The human is extraordinary" to explain how the brand had grown without any advertising during the past years. This campaign revitalized Aquarius's sales and still made the brand more human and more connected to the general public.

Think holistically.

5.1. Mainstream: Keep the Target, but Be Open to Taking Orders from New Clients

The company that launched the first modern computer was Univac. In the early 1950s, it considered its product as a computer designed for scientific work. Businesses were not considered as part of their customers or as potential customers.

On the other side, IBM was also convinced that the computer was a tool for scientists; however, they took orders from private businesses. Ten years later, Univac was still manufacturing the most advanced computer equipment, but IBM was dominating the computer market.

The market, not the entrepreneur, is the one who decides what a product will be used for. New products based on new technologies are theoretical concepts defined by entrepreneurs who always need consumer validation.

As Peter Drucker says in his book *Innovation and Entrepreneurship*, "The new venture needs to start out with the assumption may find customers in markets no one thought of, for uses no one envisaged when the product or service was designed."[34] For this reason, a new business needs to remember that customers, not a thoughtful strategy, will define the product. For that reason, any business should be open to welcome new customers to use its products.

In this case, Univac had based its business on an assumption from market research that concluded that by the year 2000, about one thousand computers would be sold. The actual number of computers sold was one million but not in the year 2000—in 1984.

Listen to and observe consumers with the intent of identifying new opportunities.

5.2. Mainstream: The Dangers of Scaling

Scaling is not only about getting bigger; it is about also improving the product and the service, improving the way a business operates, and improving the way it connects with new and existing customers. The problem comes when companies lose focus. A growing brand can lose focus in two main ways:

A. The Commodification of the Experience

On one hand, there are companies like Starbucks that forgot about the whole consumer experience and started to only look at the store growth numbers and at the scaling efficiencies.

On the other hand, there are companies like Vans, the skateboarding shoe manufacturer, that jumped into too many new markets, draining down the resources to sustain the company in the short term.

In 2007, Howard Schultz, founder of Starbucks coffee, shared his thoughts on how the company had lost its essence after growing from one thousand to thirteen thousand stores. It all was clearly underlined in the memo sent to Starbucks' ex-CEO, Jim Donald. The memo was titled "The Commoditization of the Starbucks Experience," and it spread across all publishers' desks, including those at the *Wall Street Journal*.

Starbucks didn't identify the consumer benefits that should have remained over time. For instance, Starbucks implemented new automatic espresso machines. Sure, they made operations more efficient and increased speed of service, but they also diluted the experience of coffee making. Also during those years, the coffee machine had become taller to the point that customers couldn't see how the coffee was made, at the same time making interaction with the barista more difficult. In all, those individual and little experiences vanished with expansion, watering down the Starbucks identity, a key issue that not only hurt the attractiveness of their offering but also could have left an open space for competitors focused on a premium and handcrafted coffee experience.

B. Growing in Too Many Markets

Vans also lost its focus but in a different way. In 1966, the Van Doren brothers opened the Van Doren Rubber Company in

Anaheim, California, a store that manufactured and directly sold rubber-sole shoes to the public. The company quickly found the community that valued their products most, the skateboarders. Vans had designed a unique shoe with a sticky rubber sole that became the choice of a generation of skateboarders. The Vans #44 deck shoes, now known as the Authentic, were born.

The company continued improving its product by developing a slip-on shoe with an even tighter grip. The sole had a characteristic diamond pattern, making it extremely clingy, and that would hold the feet firmly to any type of deck and surface, including those used in water sports.

During the mid-1970s, the brand's popularity exponentially grew and became a part of the skaters' and surfers' culture not only in the rest of the United States but also internationally. Their products even appeared in the iconic youth film *Fast Times at Ridgemont High* (1982) and were worn by the actor Sean Penn, who played a laidback surfer. During that period of growth, and thanks to its product innovations, Vans began to break into a considerable number of new markets, including wakeboarding, surfing, motor cross, and even athletic shoes.

The brand had entered into too many markets, expanding production facilities and extending the product lines out of their strategic focus, making the brand not as relevant to their new customers and becoming vulnerable to competitors. The tipping point and direct consequence arrived in 1983, when the company couldn't overcome its high level of debt and filed for bankruptcy.

What these two examples show is that a small brand could easily get sidetracked with new growth opportunities that drain its resources and consequently risk its sustainability. Companies should focus their efforts on identifying what makes them unique and valuable to the consumer before crossing the chasm to the mainstream market.

Focus on your core.

3.5. THE BRAND IS JUST A CONSEQUENCE

"I brand, therefore I am" has been a hallmark for decades in the advertising industry, especially during the first dot-com years.

Pets.com was one of the most iconic examples. Launched in August 1998, it had to close its doors in November 2000 due to an unproved business model and a disproportionate advertising investment in order to build a big brand. The start-up spent $11.8 million on advertising, while they were only generating $610,000 in revenues. They even created a TV ad for the Super Bowl that cost $1.2 million. To make matters worse, the ad was ranked number one by many specialized media, and they even received advertising awards. So apparently they were being applauded for their unbalanced and unstructured strategy.

What Pets.com didn't understand is that for consumers, brands are just a collection of experiences. Brands are a consequence, never a starting point. A company cannot just throw money on the table and pretend to build a big brand in a few months.

We should start to recognize a brand as a key asset in business and in marketing strategy. Ultimately, the goal is to influence consumers to select a reinvented product—an innovation—that belongs to a new category, in which our brand should be the most credible, have the most visibility, and have the highest energy to excite people so they become our customers.

Forget about building a great brand by only shouting about it through traditional advertising. Brands are not built from the top down. Brands are built strategically in an integrated way through a 360-degree approach. Every single consumer touch point contributes to the creation of a brand. That is the proven way that a small brand will get a big bite in the market.

Recognize the richness of a brand.

Part 4

FINAL CASE: GOPRO

Throughout this book, I have been sharing a structured approach to building brands that lead new categories. For this purpose, I have shared more than one hundred marketing cases to better illustrate real business situations in a new venture's evolution.

But after putting all these key experiences on paper, I believe it is useful to briefly summarize the main points of the journey of a brand until it successfully breaks into the mainstream market. To do this, I have broken down the evolution of the GoPro brand from its origins as a small brand to becoming the global and successful great brand that it is today.

If you don't know GoPro, the company designs and sells a line of wearable and mountable HD digital video cameras. GoPros are small, light, and waterproof, a design that allows one to easily capture footage from an immersive user's point of view. With this, GoPro has created a new way of shooting experiences that perfectly fits into the YouTube and social-media era.

Today, the company generates more than $1.6 billion in revenues, after increasing 16 percent year after year before 2015. In 2010, the company had fourteen employees at its head office in Half Moon Bay, California;[35] now there are more than fifteen hundred people making this small sports camera available worldwide.[36]

Reinvent
Insight of One

How did it all begin? With an insight of one. In 2002, Nick Woodman went on a surfing trip to Australia with two of his friends. The experience was so promising that Woodman felt that they needed to capture each surfing move on video. The problem was that there were only two alternatives at that time. The first option was to hire a professional photographer who got in the tube with the surfer with a wide-lens camera. However, it was expensive, and he couldn't get close enough to obtain quality pictures. The second option was to buy a disposable waterproof camera, which is very difficult to operate and took low-quality photographs.

It clearly shed light on a problem that consumers were trying to solve in an inefficient way. But there was no formal research evidence to back up Woodman's hypothesis. The inefficiency was found by practicing the sport he felt most passionate about: surfing.

Improving People's Lives with a Reinvented Solution

Woodman started to think about a possible consumer solution based on this inefficiency. First, he thought of creating a camera strap made of surf leashes. But after producing some mock-ups, he realized that it didn't really solve the consumer's problem because the camera would break and be flooded.

So he envisioned a small waterproof camera tethered to his wrist that could be affordable to the general public. The GoPro Hero was born. As Nick Woodman puts it, "I thought, what does the camera do? It helps you capture photos that make you look like a pro; it helps you capture photos that make you look like a hero."[37]

Traction

Did this solution have existing consumer traction? It certainly did. Surfers were already using waterproof cameras or traditional cameras protected by plastic cases, even though they were bulky and complex to use, with low-quality images or with no options to secure it to a surf deck. Those were the only cheaper alternatives to hiring professional photographers or buying underwater HD cameras. Consumer traction was there; the optimal solution was not.

Reinvent, Don't Invent

When Woodman created the rugged sports-camera category, he didn't invent the technology. He didn't invent the waterproof camera or the accessories to mount cameras on different surfaces.

Underwater cameras were introduced in 1957 by a Belgian inventor named Jean de Wouters, together with the French explorer Jacques Cousteau, under the name of CalypsoPhot 35mm, which later become Nikon's Nikonos camera series. Regarding camera mounts, they were first introduced in 1987 by a film producer named Mark Schulze. After learning about a new type of bike the year before in Canada, he decided to create an instructional video about mountain-biking techniques using a helmet camera. He stripped down a motorcycle helmet and installed a color video camera attached to a video recorder, including its heavy batteries—not precisely a consumer-friendly product but definitively a pioneer in this field. It was a technology that developed very quickly in the following years to the extent of coming up with a lipstick-sized camera that Formula One and NASCAR cars used to broadcast their races.

Woodman was not a pioneer. What Woodman did exceptionally well was to bring those product features together and make them affordable and easy to operate. In other words, he combined them into a product that was designed to perfectly fit the needs of surfers and other action-sports athletes. In this way, Woodman became a reinventor, because reinventors are the ones who successfully introduce new products into the mainstream market.

Create a New Category, Not a New Business
Before GoPro, there was not a sports-and-action camera category. So when GoPro launched its first camera, consumers

were not aware that they could capture their surfing and other sporting adventures. Neither were retailers expecting consumers to ask for it.

Consumer-electronics companies were not even considering creating a product for this limited use and for the small surfing community. Industry leaders were too obsessed with increasing the number of pixels and adding bells and whistles to their digital cameras. What those large companies did not expect was that in the following years, the mobile phone would replace the point-and-shoot camera market, consequently shrinking their core category.

Define the New Category with Focused Innovation

Remember what Herb Kelleher, CEO of Southwest Airlines, told a marketing executive: "I can teach you the secret to running this airline business in thirty seconds. This is it: we are *the* low-fare airline. Once you understand that fact, you can make any decision about this company's future as well as I can. So does your proposal help the business to become the unchallenged low-fare airline? Because if it doesn't, we're not serving any damn chicken salad."

A company that establishes a new category has to define and focus on the main driver that will build credibility and consideration among a group of customers. Keep the main thing the main thing. Every decision you make needs to get the business closer to achieving its unique value to the customer.

Strategically, GoPro wisely focused its resources to own the surfing and action-sports category, a decision that protected the business from competitors coming from different angles: mobile phones trying to capture the casual photography market and eating away at point-and-shoot cameras, and the leading imaging and optical companies, such as Canon or Nikon, trying to capture the high-end digital single-lens reflex (DSLR) market.

Build a Core Advantage

To maintain its leadership position in the sports-camera category, GoPro needed to gain a core advantage over its rivals by creating a barrier to entry so that it would be much more difficult for competitors to imitate GoPro's business model and its unique set of operations. That is why it is so critically important that the new solution you create resides at the core of your organization.

Although GoPro might appear to have gained its core advantage by designing its software and hardware components (which include image silicon processors, new image sensors, and lenses), it has also gained power through its community-oriented and content strategy. The company encourages and rewards GoPro camera users for sharing their compelling content on social media such as Facebook, Instagram, and YouTube. Its official YouTube channel has attracted over 3.8 million subscribers and more than 1.1 billion views by featuring videos that are uploaded by its customers and influential athletes.

By doing so, GoPro has turned its customers into a community of fans by inspiring others to believe that they, too, can "be the hero" by using a GoPro camera to record and share their experiences.

<u>Don't Overprotect—Invest in Continuous Innovation</u>
The innovation machine should never stop. GoPro has continuously been launching improved versions of its iconic HD Hero camera and new accessories to serve the following four purposes:

1. *Building a Product Portfolio:*
   By launching new products, a company can immediately reduce the price of its previous model. In this way, brands create a balanced product portfolio with more affordable products that will be used as a new entry point to the brand for consumers. At the same time, new models will drive new purchases from already existing GoPro customers who are looking for the latest technology.

2. *Creating New, Relevant, and Unique Products:*
   A product is never really finished. Companies have to introduce new technologies and integrate customers' feedback to make it a better product. In the case of GoPro, it all changed when they launched their first high-definition video camera in 2009. In the following months, sales skyrocketed; at the same pace, users flooded YouTube and Facebook with their own videos.

3. *Making New Occasions:*
   By launching a new line of mounts, the company ensured that consumers would be able to capture their experiences on more occasions, not only while surfing but also while skiing or riding a bike, thus creating a new source of revenue that is incremental to the

business and that does not cannibalize any of the core products.

4. *Blocking Competitors:*
A company cannot stop once it has produced a winning product because competitors will try to steal share from the category it has created. This is not something that *could* happen. This is something that *will* actually happen if your company is growing and the consumer and industry buzz starts to spread.

Even disruptive brands like GoPro need to continue innovating to defend themselves against new competitors like Contour, Memoto, or Autographer and existing consumer-electronics companies that will try to clone the original product. GoPro acquired a leading digital-video software company called CineForm in 2011. It recently released a rig that allowed consumers to record in 3-D by putting two cameras together that shoot at the same time. It has also released a Wi-Fi plug-in that enables users to easily upload pictures and video from the camera to the computer. And the GoPro innovation machine will not stop.

Build
Start Small, but Do Start
Any project can seem too big at the beginning, especially when you are trying to build a game-changing action-sports camera from scratch. For that reason, Woodman began with small steps that could allow him to launch his idea with limited

resources, with less experience in the industry, but in faster time than any of his competitors.

When Woodman returned to California in 2002 from his trip to Australia, he spent three months selling bead-and-shell belts, which he had bought in Indonesia at music festivals and flea markets. With the profits and a family loan, he began sewing his first prototypes of clothing straps to fit a portable camera. The straps worked fine; the issue was that the camera was not prepared for underwater and extreme use. Water got into the camera and damaged it. So Woodman clearly saw that he should not build a strap company. The only way of capturing the underwater and sports-camera market and solving his consumer problem was by building a camera company.

GoPro's original camera used 35mm film, when at that time all the market was moving to digital. Given the fact that Woodman did not have the skills to create a 3-D model using a computer, he just built the product prototype with his own hands. He only needed a Dremel tool, plastic, and some glue. He mailed a conceptual design to a Chinese manufacturer that produced reusable cameras for snorkelers so that they could produce the first product line, taking into account his limited budget of $5,000.

Design Should Simplify

GoPro's first camera was not what it is today, an HD video camera with dozens of accessories to mount it on any vehicle or surface. The first camera took photos only and had two buttons, one to switch on the camera and the other one to record. Also, it allowed consumers to set interval records so that the camera could take snapshots every two, five, ten, thirty, or sixty seconds. The product was designed to simplify the way people took photographs while practicing surfing. It was designed for the extremes, for the heavy users who would value these product features the most.

Besides, this allowed the company to concentrate all its resources on fewer but better-working product features. It was a cheap and fast way of launching the product and getting feedback from consumers and retailers.

Throughout the years, the company has evolved but has always maintained its simplicity and focus on creating the best action-sports camera in the market.

Engage
The Fall of Advertising to Build a Brand

Relying on traditional advertising and mass media to build a small brand is not the most effective strategy; lack of credibility, media fragmentation, and high costs have become staggering challenges for marketing executives and entrepreneurs.

The key to overcoming those barriers is to master new media channels that enable a higher level of engagement with customers in order to get more relevant eyeballs than investing in traditional channels. GoPro's answer to that challenge was to create an all-year-round content marketing strategy that has made the brand a household name.

But GoPro hasn't been content to rest on its laurels as one of YouTube's "Top 10 Brands." In fact, the company has embraced content so heartily that it wants to be much more than a hardware company. GoPro wants to evolve into the user-generated media company of the future.

As Adam Dornbusch, GoPro's head of content distribution, said at *Variety*'s Entertainment and Technology Summit, "The camera is just the tool to get to content."

<u>Find a Niche Community</u>

> *The first thing we get excited about isn't what will this do for our business from a revenue standpoint—or, really, from any traditional business standpoint. It's how stoked are our customers and fans.*

—TOM FOSTER, THE GOPRO ARMY[38]

Woodman invited his roommate and friend, Neil Dana, to join the project and help him with sales. Given the superior set of benefits of the rugged and waterproof camera to the surfers' community, Woodman and Dana focused on calling and visiting all the surf retailers across the country to get their cameras on the shelves. The successful approach resulted in $350,000 revenue by the end of 2005, their first year in business.

Not only was the camera a user-centric device, but also the way GoPro connected and engaged with consumers was extremely focused on them. GoPro established a self-expressive and emotional higher purpose for its brand that was relevant to the target community. GoPro became a brand that allowed people to document their lives and share them online. There were thousands of people around the world sharing their experiences and communicating among themselves thanks to GoPro. That is much bigger than just selling cameras for surfing. And for the people watching the online content, it quickly became an aspiring brand closely associated with an adventurous lifestyle.

Grassroots Marketing
Advertising won't make a difference in a company's launching phase because it does not convey a credible or an authentic message. New ventures need to start from the ground up, the way GoPro did when connecting with retailers and consumers.

The company attended trade shows and spread its message in a commando style, saying that it would give away cameras to people who shouted, "GoPro! GoPro! GoPro!" the loudest. This was one of their first stunts that made people wonder what was going on with GoPro. This strategy allowed them to list their products in two major retailers, Dick's Sporting Goods and REI. In the following months, moving into positive evolution, other retailers like Best Buy gave the new brand a shot. Later that year, Best Buy awarded GoPro for becoming a top new supplier.

To connect with consumers, GoPro initiated a two-way strategy. First, it began creating breathtaking content that people wanted to watch and share. Second, it initiated a sponsorship program for action-sports athletes, a program built to increase the visibility of the cameras within the extreme-sports community, thanks to being associated with pro athletes and their flawless performances. It's a platform that has grown over time to today, accumulating more than seventy athletes.

Viral Inflection Point

One identity trait that GoPro cultivated from the beginning was to create unique action-sports content. Not only did GoPro create professional and original content, but customers also filmed eye-catching videos and shared them online. It was more about sharing the content rather than keeping the videos for oneself. For this reason, content marketing presented a huge viral potential from a strategic viewpoint.

Woodman soon realized that following this content strategy had increased the brand's visibility and consideration more than anything else they were doing. It soon became the driving force of GoPro.

From a competitive point of view, this viral strategy separated GoPro from any of its existing competitors in terms of brand personality and sales performance, including outcompeting the Contour sports and mountable camera that was launched in 2004, the same year Woodman began testing the first versions of his camera.

Since GoPro implemented the content strategy in 2007, together with the launch of its first digital video camera, the HD Hero 3, this allowed the company to accelerate its growth rate and set it apart from competitors. In 2006, the camera reached sales of $800,000. In 2007, after the HD Hero 3 launch, the new product brought in $3.4 million, more than quadrupling the figure from the previous year.

In the following years, GoPro continued to innovate by launching its first HD digital video camera in 2010 and by adding new mounts to broaden its number of applications, new products that grew its customer and fan base. For instance, they went from fifty thousand Facebook fans to more than 1.3 million in 2011 alone, while Contour had only reached fifty-six thousand fans at the end of 2011. By the end of 2012, GoPro's sales were more than $520 million, and it is estimated that in 2013 the company achieved $1 billion in revenue.

What GoPro understood from the beginning is that thousands of passionate fans talking about its product was much more credible and authentic than creating traditional ads that only try to sell the technical superiority of a product.

The Brand Is Just a Consequence

What Woodman started as a project to create a camera strap for surfing ended up as the leading HD action camera in the world, enabling sports professionals, the military, scientists, and even TV producers to use it on a daily basis.

In October 2012, when Felix Baumgartner jumped from 128,100 feet above the earth's surface, people from all over the world could watch this iconic event thanks to having seven GoPro cameras attached to his body, documenting every moment. In 2010, when the Chilean miners were rescued, a GoPro camera was used to transmit the live footage.

GoPro, as the ultimate reinventor, has become one of the biggest brands worldwide and has maintained its position as a leader—a direct consequence of having created a unique solution for a community of passionate users, of managing the sports-camera category it created, of constantly innovating and delivering unique solutions, and of engaging with its customers through content like no other brand has ever done before.

Part 5

FINAL THOUGHTS

An old Sioux legend tells that one evening, next to the bonfire of the camp, a chief Cherokee of a tribe gathered all his grandsons around to share a story about life. This is how it starts:

There is one battle that goes on inside people.

He said, "My son, the battle is between two wolves inside us all. One is evil. It is anger, envy, jealousy, sorrow, regret, greed, arrogance, self-pity, guilt, resentment, inferiority, lies, false pride, superiority, and ego. The other is good. It is joy, peace, love, hope, serenity, humility, kindness, benevolence, empathy, generosity, truth, compassion and faith."

The grandson thought about it for a minute and then asked his grandfather, "Which wolf wins?"

The old Cherokee simply replied, "The one you feed."

This battle illustrates the choice every executive or entrepreneur faces. One can choose to be an incumbent: defensive, predictable, and focused on market share, on the past, and on seeking average growth through incremental improvements. Or one can choose to be the reinventor: game-changing, dynamic, unexpected, and focused on creating new categories, on creating new brand territories, and on seeking disruptive growth through creating relevant and unique consumer solutions that matter.

You will become the one you feed. So if you choose to become the reinventor, you will need to acquire the knowledge and experience needed for the successful practice of reinvention.

With this book, I have aimed to push further the knowledge frontier in the field of marketing and innovation and to inspire you to make something that matters. I hope I have made some contribution to it. But now it is your goal to narrow the gap between knowledge and experience by practicing reinvention and by implementing an innovation culture in your organization that enables it to disrupt industries and achieve growth by challenging the status quo.

ACKNOWLEDGMENTS

I consider this book as something beyond a three-year research and creative project. This book summarizes all my professional experience as a marketer and entrepreneur. For this reason, it would not have been possible without all the experiences and learning that I got from the following extraordinary people I have been grateful to work with. So I thank them for their support, encouragement, energy, insight, and friendship: Linda Kreitzman, Greg Madigan, Roger Lord, Dan Sear, Ruth Barker, Roberto Torri, Brenda del Val, Julia Sanchez, Pere Puig, Eva Gispert, Carlos Salas, Enrique Dans, José María Castillejo, and Ismael Pascual.

To my family, especially Cristina, a heartfelt thank-you, which not only has to do with this book but also with everything to do with your inspiration and unconditional support in all that I do.

ABOUT THE AUTHOR

Roger Cusa is a marketing director with experience in managing consumer brands, leading innovation projects and teams, and developing new ways of connecting and engaging with consumers through marketing campaigns.

He has spent more than fifteen years launching and managing global brands in the QSR industry and in FMCG multinationals such as Subway, Burger King, Ferrero Group, Mapa Spontex, and Flamagas. As an entrepreneur, he founded and managed the digital and branding agency Episodius.

In 2011, he published the book *Crea Tu Proyecto Tube* (Lid Editorial), which established the foundations of YouTube and online video as a strategic marketing tool for brands.

His writing and work on marketing have appeared in The Food and Drink Innovation Network, Marketing Week, International Digital Content Forum, Quick Service Restaurant Media, Campaign, The Grocer, La Vanguardia,

El Economista, Emprendedores, La Información, Telecinco, TVE, and Antena 3.

Cusa holds an international MBA from IE Business School with a Fellow Award in marketing, a master's degree in marketing with distinction and first-class honors from the University of California at Berkeley, and an executive diploma in strategic marketing and technology from Stanford University.

END NOTES

1   Jerry Weintraub, "His Way, a portrait of Hollywood legend Jerry Weintraub", directed by Douglas McGrath, aired March 4, 2011. USA: HBO Documentary Films.

2   Gigi Padovani, *Nutella: Un mito italiano* (Milano, IT: Rizzoli, 2004).

3   Edmund S. Phelps, *Mass Flourishing: How Grassroots Innovation Created Jobs, Challenge, and Change* (Princeton: Princeton University Press, 2015).

4   Andrew S. Grove, *Only the Paranoid Survive* (New York: Doubleday Business, 1996).

5   Albert Om, "El Convidat: Ferran Adria" television interview series, Televisió de Catalunya/ August 26, 2013. TV3, Barcelona, http://www.ccma.cat/tv3/alacarta/el-convidat/ferran-adria/video/4373490/.

6   Sony Corporation 50th Anniversary Project Team, *"Genryu: Sony 50th Anniversary"*, (Tokyo, Japan: Sony Corporation, 1996).

7   Faith Popcorn and Lys Marigold, *Clicking* (New York: Harper Collins Publishers Inc., 1996).

8   Jesse L. Lasky, *I Blow My Own Horn* (New York: Doubleday & Co, 1957).

9   Dan Mitchell, "These Are the Top 5 Energy Drinks," *Time*, May 11, 2015, http://time.com/3854658/these-are-the-top-5-energy-drinks/.

10 David Aaker, *Brand Relevance: Making Competitors Irrelevant* (San Francisco: Jossey-Bass, 2011).

11 Edmund Phelps, *Mass Flourishing: How Grassroots Innovation Created Jobs, Challenge, and Change* (Princeton: Princeton University Press, 2015).

12 Theodore Levitt, *Innovative imitation*, (Harvard College: Harvard Business Review, September/October issue, 1966).

13 Mark Cuban, "Only Morons Start a Business on a Loan," TV interview, Bloomberg Business, June 14, 2013, https://youtu.be/KYneLGRTgy8.

14 David Sheff, *Game Over: Press to Start to Continue* (Wilton, CT: Cyberactive, 1999).

15 Steven L. Kent, *The First Quarter: A 25 Year History of Video Games* (Colorado Springs, CO: BWD Press, 2000).

16 David Sheff, *Game Over: Press to Start to Continue* (Wilton, CT: Cyberactive, 1999).

17 Steven P. Schnaars, *Managing Imitation Strategies* (New York: Free Press, 2002).

18 Andrew S. Grove, *Only the Paranoid Survive* (New York: Doubleday Business, 1996).

19 Steven P. Schnaars, *Managing Imitation Strategies* (New York: Free Press, 2002).

20 Steven P. Schnaars, *Managing Imitation Strategies* (New York: Free Press, 2002).

21 James M. Utterback, *Mastering the Dynamics of Innovation* (Boston, Mass: Harvard Business School Press, 1994).

22 Marty Neumeier, Marty Neumeier's Innovation Workshop: Brand Strategy + Design Thinking = Transformation (DVD), directed by Marty Neumeier aired 2010. San Francisco, CA: New Riders.

23 Tarmo Virki, "Nokia's Cheap Phone Tops Electronics Chart", *Reuters UK*, May 3, 2007, http://uk.reuters.com/article/us-nokia-history-idUKL0262945620070503.

24 Navi Radjou and Jaideep Prabhu, *Jugaad Innovation: Think Frugal, Be Flexible, Generate Breakthrough Growth* (San Francisco, CA: Jossey-Bass, A Wiley Imprint, 2012).

25 Navi Radjou and Jaideep Prabhu, *Jugaad Innovation: Think Frugal, Be Flexible, Generate Breakthrough Growth* (San Francisco, CA: Jossey-Bass, A Wiley Imprint, 2012).

26 Kotoe Oshima, "Plastic Bottles Light Up Lives," *CNN World*, August 30, 2011, http://edition.cnn.com/2011/WORLD/asiapcf/08/30/eco.philippines.bottle/Kate McGeown, "How Water Bottles Create Cheap Lighting in Philippines," *BBC News*, September 18, 2011, http://www.bbc.com/news/world-asia-pacific-14967535.

27 Sydney Ember, "Digital Ad Spending Expected to Soon Surpass TV," *New York Times*, December 7, 2015, http://www.nytimes.com/2015/12/07/business/media/digital-ad-spending-expected-to-soon-surpass-tv.html.

28 Phil Knight, "Swoosh! Inside Nike" documentary, directed by CNBC, aired 2008. CNBC production: CNBC.

29 Business 2.0 magazine writers, "Hits and Myths," *Business 2.0* magazine, September 2000.

30 Eric Ries, *The Lean Startup: How Today's Entrepreneurs Use Continuous Innovation to Create Radically Successful Business* (New York: Crown Business, 2011).

31 Bill Taylor, "It's More Important to Be Kind than Clever," *Harvard Business Review*, August 23, 2012, https://hbr.org/2012/08/its-more-important-to-be-kind.

32 United States Department of Agriculture writers, "Citrus: World Markets and Trade", January 2016, https://apps.fas.usda.gov/psdonline/circulars/citrus.pdf.

33 People magazine writers, "Just Tickled," *People* magazine, January 13, 1997. http://www.people.com/people/archive/article/0,,20143226,00.html.

34 Peter F. Drucker, *Innovation and Entrepreneurship* (New York: Harper & Row, 1985).

35 Tom Foster, "The GoPro Army," *Inc. Magazine*, January 26, 2012, http://www.inc.com/magazine/201202/the-gopro-army.html.

36 Acquire Media writers, "GoPro Announces Q4 and Calendar Year 2015 Preliminary Results," January 13, 2016, http://investor.gopro.com/releasedetail.cfm?releaseid=950216.

37 Dan Ashley, "Inspiration from GoPro Camera Came During Surfing Trip," ABC News, November 15, 2012, http://abc-7news.com/archive/8887336/.

38 Tom Foster, "The GoPro Army," *Inc. Magazine*, January 26, 2012, http://www.inc.com/magazine/201202/the-gopro-army.html.

17324926R00147

Printed in Poland
by Amazon Fulfillment
Poland Sp. z o.o., Wrocław